If You Like Us,
Talk About Us

If You Like Us, Talk About Us

The Life and Times of
ROBERT H. PORTERFIELD

The Founder of Virginia's World-Famous Barter Theatre

Robert L. McKinney

Barter
Media

For Lynn,
My muse always and forever

© 2006 Robert L. McKinney

Interior pages by Craig Hines, Bellerophon Productions
Cover design by Stefan Killen Design, New York, NY
Cover portrait by Jan Clausing

First edition

Published by Barter Media
Abingdon, Virginia

This book is printed on acid-free paper that meets the American National Standards Institute Z39.48 standard. ⊗

PRINTED IN THE UNITED STATES OF AMERICA

11 10 09 08 07 06   6 5 4 3 2 1

Publisher's Cataloging-in-Publication
(Provided by Quality Books, Inc.)

McKinney, Robert L., 1946–
    If you like us, talk about us : the life and times of Robert H. Porterfield, the founder of Virginia's world-famous Barter Theatre / Robert L. McKinney.

    p. cm.
    Includes index.
    ISBN-13: 978-0-9789142-0-2 (hardcover)
    ISBN-10: 0-9789142-0-1 (hardcover)
    ISBN-13: 978-0-9789142-1-9 (pbk.)
    ISBN-10: 0-9789142-1-X (pbk.)

1. Porterfield, Robert, 1905–1971. 2. Theatrical managers — Virginia — Biography. 3. Barter Theatre — History — 20th century. 4. Theaters — Virginia — Abingdon — History — 20th century. 5. Abingdon (Va.) — History — 20th century. I. Title.

PN2277.A242B378 2006
792'.092   QBI06-600386

Contents

Foreword

From childhood we all have dreams, yet many of us lack the courage and determination to make our dreams come true. As children we dream of someday becoming a fireman, policeman, lawyer, doctor, nurse, or dancer but as we grow older our dreams change. Robert Porterfield's childhood dream was of the Theatre—to be an actor. His dream never changed but intensified with each passing year. He was determined to be an actor so, despite all odds, he left college and went to New York to attend the American Academy of Dramatic Arts.

This book brings out the joys, the sorrows, and the struggles that Robert Porterfield experienced while fulfilling his dream. He faced many obstacles, including the Depression of the early 1930s, but his faith and love for the Theatre grew stronger every day. He wanted to make people forget, if only for a few hours, their day-to-day lives by becoming lost in his fantasy world. This he accomplished, despite the Depression, by bringing a group of hungry, unemployed actors to his beloved Southwest Virginia. Here he realized his dream and founded the Barter Theatre in 1933.

Robert Porterfield will be remembered for his wonderful smile, his spontaneous laughter, and his effervescent personality. His accomplishments and awards were many. One memory that will never fade was the way he shared a part of himself with his audience before each play. He gave a little speech, told a little story, and made everyone laugh. When the curtain was ready to open and he had everyone in the palm of his hand, he would smile the smile of a man whose dream had come true and say, "If you like us, talk about us. And if you don't, just keep your mouth shut."

Mary Dudley Porterfield

Twin Oaks
September 19, 2006

Acknowledgments

The idea of writing a biography of Robert Porterfield was first suggested to me a couple of years ago by Barter Theatre and Dr. David Wilkin, the president of Virginia Highlands Community College in Abingdon. At first there was talk of possible grant funding for the project or for hiring a research assistant, but when cash failed to materialize I decided that if Bob Porterfield could start a theatre on faith, I could certainly write a book on it.

Barter Theatre threw open its extensive archives to me without any restrictions, including the distinct privilege of digging through boxes and boxes of old photographs, playbills, newspaper clippings, and more than half a century of Barter memorabilia. Barter's producing artistic director Richard Rose; staff members Debbie Addison, Lisa Alderman, and Jayne Duehring; and many others have been especially helpful. Many thanks also to Bob Land, eagle-eyed copyeditor and book packager, without whose enthusiasm, expertise, and knowledge we'd still be wondering what to do first.

Robert Porterfield's widow Mary Dudley Porterfield, a wonderful Southern Lady—and the capital letters are fully intended—shared her vast knowledge of both Bob Porterfield and Barter Theatre in many honest and invigorating conversations at Twin Oaks, the Porterfield homeplace near Glade Spring, Virginia. She also allowed the use of numerous photographs never before published.

Much of the information presented here has been taken directly from *Patron Saint of the Impossible*, an unpublished autobiography that Bob Porterfield completed in, as far as can be told, the early 1960s. He may have been assisted in this project by a professional writer, possibly a Pat Hale, but I have not been able to confirm this, and I have been unable to locate her. Almost all of the quotes attributed to Bob have been lifted directly from this wonderful primary source. Mary Dudley holds the copyright on this manuscript, and with her permission, many of the passages have been paraphrased, often using Bob Porterfield's own descriptions of events, places, and his own feelings to the point that he must be considered at least a coauthor. Bob's manuscript, although a primary source and quite interesting, is stuffed full of far too many obscure yet important names to be very readable for the general public. Hopefully it may someday see publication or, at the very least, be photocopied and made available to Theatre historians and researchers.

Another fine resource has been Anne St. Clair Williams's 1970 doctoral thesis "Robert Porterfield's Barter Theatre of Abingdon, Virginia: The State Theatre of Virginia," copyrighted in 1971. The copy of her thesis (University of Illinois at Urbana–Champaign) was purchased from UMI Dissertation Services, 777 Eisenhower Parkway, POB 1346, Ann Arbor, MI 48106-1346.

The Barter Theatre Story: Love Made Visible by Mark Dawidziak, published in 1982 by the Appalachian Consortium Press in Boone, North Carolina, also proved very useful, as were several long telephone conversations with Mark, during which he added greatly to the author's store of Barter knowledge.

Many others shared their memories of Bob Porterfield and offered suggestions of items for investigation. Among these, specific acknowledgment should go to Ben and Merry Jennings, Dr. French Moore Jr., Eddie Yates, Pearl Hayter, the historical societies of both Wythe and Washington (Virginia) counties, and the librarians of the Smyth-Bland Regional Library in Marion, the Washington County Public Library in Abingdon, and those members of the reference department of the Bristol Public Library. Thanks are also due to Dean Roark, whose daddy used to drive the Barter buses. Some of Dean's daddy's tales, although they might make delicious reading, may have been embellished just a tiny bit and are therefore best left in the oral tradition.

This book is accurate to the very best of the author's knowledge but is not represented as a work of pure scholarship. Instead, the hope is that it will be an enjoyable and informative read about a marvelous and unique individual.

Questions of source material or quotes have been, as far as is possible, dealt with in the text or in parentheses, thereby avoiding the use of more scholarly forms of documentation. The thesis of Williams and the book by Dawidziak include many additional references.

Sugar Grove, Virginia
July 2006

Author's Note

A few of Bob Porterfield's words or stereotypes quoted may seem by today's standards to be insulting, politically incorrect, or archaic. For example, he cites his Scottish ancestors as being frugal and conservative, refers to Native Americans as "Indians," credits some of his creativity and love of music and theatre to his bit of Irish blood, and refers to his first wife's "Pennsylvania Dutch" family as hardworking and conservative. The one really glaring example, however, and the inclusion of which has caused the most criticism from early readers of this book is the word "Negro" and, in one quote, the word "colored." Neither word was considered derogatory at the time it was used, and Bob Porterfield, of all people, would never have used any word or phrase that insulted people because of their race. A standard writing technique when wishing to expunge an insulting word is to leave out the word and insert another in brackets: for example, substituting "[African American]" for "Negro," but then some readers might conclude that Bob used another, far less acceptable word, which he would not have done. Bob Porterfield, when he judged people at all, did so solely on their moral character, their ability, and their willingness to work hard— not on things such as skin color, over which none of us has any control. In fact, Barter Theatre never in its history practiced any form of segregation, although that was the accepted practice all the way up to 1965 in movie theaters, public transportation, and even schools.

Introduction

This is a story about the Theatre and particularly about one man, Robert Huffard Porterfield, who had himself a very fine dream, about how he made his dream come true, and how that most excellent dream took on a life of its own that will far outlast any individual.

Bob Porterfield's dream—of which the bricks and mortar, nails and two-by-fours, sets and props and lights, wigs, costumes, and jars of makeup, stagehands, janitors, house managers, sellers of fudge and souvenirs, ushers and ticket folks, scripts, and actors are only a small part—is Virginia's deservedly world-famous Barter Theatre in the brick-sidewalked and genteel little hamlet of Abingdon.

Located on the old Wilderness Road, Abingdon has always attracted pioneers. Originally known as Black's Fort after a fellow named Black who built a stockade in the wilderness, Abingdon was later called Wolf Hills because Daniel Boone camped there on one of his longhunting forays and fought off a pack of wolves that came out of a cavern and attacked his dogs. Its streets have reverberated to the tread of soldiers on their way to the American Revolution's Battle of Kings Mountain, the tramp of hobnailed boots worn by both Confederate and Yankee soldiers during the War Between the States, the rattle of stagecoach wheels, the grinding rumble of ox-drawn wagons, and even the gobbling of thousand-bird flocks of turkeys being driven to market. It is a shade-dappled town with lots of huge old oak and maple trees, and in the springtime the air smells of dogwood blossoms and the freshly turned earth of little backyard gardens.

Note that this book, as did Bob Porterfield, spells "Theatre" with the more formal "re" rather than "er." This treatment is, of course, entirely on purpose and intended. "Theatre," spelled thus, and often with the first letter capitalized, can well be defined as, to use the words of the *New Oxford American Dictionary*, "the activity or profession of acting in, producing, directing, or writing plays." This is altogether different from "theater," which is better described—

not necessarily by Oxford—as a building reeking of stale butter-soggy popcorn and spilled soda pop in which movies, politicians, and professional wrestlers may be observed.

Allow a few minutes as we set the scenery for our play and give a bit of the backstory to provide a good understanding of the characters you're about to meet. "So-and-so begat so-and-so" is pretty boring stuff to read, but it will be held to a minimum. Readers who endure it will be rewarded with drama, comedy, romance, excitement, poignancy, and everything else that live Theatre is capable of creating. For those folks who want more genealogy and history instead of less, *The Porterfields* by Frank B. Porterfield should keep them happy for hours puzzling out family lines. This book is long out of print but can be found through interlibrary loan; the Historical Society of Washington County, Virginia, has a copy one can read.

Bob Porterfield—as he was known by his friends, which included just about everybody who ever knew him—treated the dirt farmers of Appalachia with the same interest and respect that he gave presidents and First Ladies and world-renowned actors. It might better be said that he accorded the rich and famous as much respect, or almost as much, as he gave to hardworking laborers, hardscrabble farmers, barefoot mountaineers, and other folks who have good, honest dirt under their fingernails.

He was an undeniably handsome man who stood just over six feet tall with a fine head of hair and a large smile that could light up any room he was in like a bank of eight-inch Fresnel spotlights. He was far, far larger than life, and yet a more down-to-earth and humble human being has perhaps never trod the cracked asphalt of Broadway or the stingy soil of a Virginia hillside. He called nearly everybody, men and women alike, "Honey," and he meant it.

Often, sitting in the magical darkness of Barter Theatre, one cannot deny that Bob Porterfield's warm and friendly spirit is there as well. Chatting with his marvelous Lady, Mary Dudley Porterfield, at their beloved antebellum home known as Twin Oaks, one is fully aware of Bob's invisible hand on the visitor's shoulder.

Robert Huffard Porterfield was born on December 21, 1905, on the outskirts of Austinville, in Wythe County, Virginia. He was the third of six children born to William Breckenridge Porterfield and

Daisy Huffard Porterfield, who were married on November 20, 1901. (Samuel H. Porterfield, the second child, was born on December 9, 1904, but died on January 11, 1905.) Bob's oldest brother, Lilburn Breckenridge Porterfield, was born in 1903. Lilburn and Robert would be followed by three more children: Albert Graham Porterfield, born in 1909; William B. Porterfield II, born in 1911; and Frank Argyle Porterfield, born in 1914.

The six sons of William B. Porterfield were fifth-generation Americans. Their great-great-great-grandfather arrived in the American colonies from Scotland in about 1760, probably through the port of Philadelphia. The exact date and entry point are somewhat fuzzy, and there is even a little bit of confusion about his given name. It was more than likely John, but then again could have been Frank. Like many immigrants of Scots, Irish, Scots-Irish, or German descent, he traveled from Pennsylvania down the lush and fertile Shenandoah Valley only to find all of the best land already staked out and occupied, forcing him to keep pushing on until he arrived at some unclaimed real estate in Southwest Virginia.

According to Porterfield family legend, he was a man small of stature but long of life, reportedly living to the age of 102. Nothing at all seems to be known of his wife, not even her name. Upon the death of John or Frank, all of his family except one son, John, abandoned Southwest Virginia for Pennsylvania.

John married a widow Brooks, whose maiden name had been Kincannon. She and John had five children, two boys and three girls. An explorer of sorts, John is said to have been the first man to drive a wagon through Keywood's Gap in Walker Mountain, Virginia. Their second son, James, was born in 1791. Bob Porterfield's generous serving of the blarney came to him through his Kincannon Irish forebears, or so he liked to claim.

James served as a soldier in the War of 1812, then, in 1819, married Jennettie Clark, the daughter of James and Isabella Breckenridge Clark. James and Jennettie had eight children, the fifth being Lilburn, who was born on September 26, 1830.

Lilburn Breckenridge Porterfield married Rachel Buchanan in 1854. Their seventh child (of eight) was William Breckenridge Porterfield, born in 1875. He married Daisy Huffard on November

20, 1901, in the parlor of her home in Wytheville, Virginia. In the newspaper parlance of the day, he was a "thrifty and popular young farmer," and his bride was "the charming eldest daughter of Mr. S. B. Huffard."

The Huffards had long been prominent Wythe (pronounced "with" and named after George Wythe, a signer of the Declaration of Independence) and Tazewell county citizens. Daisy Huffard brought her own interesting lineage into the marriage that would produce Robert Huffard Porterfield, but it is unfortunately very difficult to ferret out much detailed information about female ancestors other than their dates of birth (usually) and death, that they married so-and-so, and how many children they bore. Quite often, as noted above, not even their names were recorded, and it was far from uncommon for men of the frontier days to outlive several wives. Pioneer women often died young from childbirth complications, overwork, disease, or malnutrition.

Bob Porterfield's great-great-great-grandmother on his mother's side was more than likely responsible for a small streak of Cherokee blood that joined the Scots and Irish in his veins. Just about every Appalachian person one meets claims to have an "Indian princess" somewhere in his or her lineage (although Native Americans didn't actually have princesses, as such), but claiming a Native American male as an ancestor is highly unusual. Apparently it was considered acceptable for a Caucasian Lothario to romance a dusky-skinned Native American woman, but not the other way around. However, as Bob Porterfield told it:

> Early in her marriage, according to the family story, she had been abducted by a tribe of Cherokee Indians and disappeared into the wilderness. Her husband tried desperately to find out where they had taken her, sending out scouts and anxiously questioning every traveler, but it was five months before he learned that she and her captors had crossed the river and gone into the adjacent territory of what is now Kentucky. He followed after, and some weeks later arrived in the camp, bearing his saddlebags full of trinkets and beads to barter back his bride.
>
> He was successful, and carried her back to the family homestead. Several months later she gave birth to my great-

great-grandfather. All she would ever say about the matter was simply, "My, my, I must have been raped by an Indian."

I didn't hear this story until much later, because my mother would never speak of it, but my earliest recollections are of the high cheekbones and proud carriage that she bore as the stamp of her Cherokee heritage.

Although born on the Porterfield homeplace, Twin Oaks, just outside Glade Spring, Virginia, William B. Porterfield about 1900 became lands overseer for the New Jersey Zinc Company in Austinville in Wythe County. Austinville, birthplace of Stephen F. Austin, the "Father of Texas," was at the transition from the nineteenth to the twentieth century a small village on the banks of the New River, which, most geologists agree, is the world's second-oldest existing river. Austinville proper was located on the north bank of the river with the mining camp occupying a ridgetop safely removed about a half-mile to the south. This arm's-length suburb of Austinville was a typical company town with everything owned and controlled by the New Jersey Zinc Company. There was a company store where company scrip paid to the company workers in lieu of cash could be spent and a charge account maintained, a company infirmary with a company-supplied doctor and nurse, company housing for the miners and their families, a company school with a company-provided teacher, a company-built church, and other company facilities and services that served, exploited, and enslaved the laborers. In addition to zinc and other minerals, lead was a major product of the Austinville mines. Lead dust, as well as the chemicals such as mercury used to extract metal from the ore, was known even a century ago as highly toxic to human health, but few if any precautions were taken to protect the mostly illiterate and often foreign-born miners because such laborers were more or less looked upon as being expendable.

One story, perhaps apocryphal, relates that a company supervisor once ordered some workers to go into a new section of mine to test the air to see if it was safe to breathe. When asked by the miners why he didn't just send in one of the mules that pulled the ore cars, he informed them, "I can always hire more miners; a mule I'd have to buy!"

The lands overseer for New Jersey Zinc's Austinville holdings, however, was a far more valued employee, more respected and better paid—in cash. The company owned thousands of acres of property overlying the minerals below and utilized them for a variety of purposes, including timbering, farming, and livestock production. As lands overseer, William Porterfield was entitled to live in a large antebellum home known as the Old Fulton Farmhouse located about a mile away from the central mine and ore-processing operation and the rows of tiny, identical company houses.

It was almost certainly in this farmhouse that William and Daisy's second son, Robert Huffard Porterfield, was born. Although no records positively place Robert Porterfield's birth at home, in 1905 the rare delivery occurred anywhere else. His entry into the world may or may not have been attended by a doctor. Few births were in those days, but the mining camp did have a company physician, and William Porterfield was, after all, the equivalent of what would today be called middle management.

Undoubtedly a midwife or two were present at Bob Porterfield's birth, and a safe assumption is that an African American wet nurse stood at the ready should the need for her services occur, that practice being common in that place and those days. In fact, Bob Porterfield himself would many years later write about his "Negro mammy," a lady named Mary Trueheart:

> Certainly no boy could have had a greater privilege than to have had my black mammy. My mother must have had a gift for timing, for Black Mammy always had a baby along about the time that she did, and when we were three or four months old we were turned over to her as our wet nurse. Along with her good, rich "colored" milk, she provided us boys with a great deal of love and joy. Mary Trueheart was her name, and I don't think anybody ever lived up to a name as well as she did. She was black as the ace of spades, with shiny white teeth and a crystal-clear sense of what was good and true and honest.

Although astrology cannot be scientifically proven any more than any other myth or religion, the date of Robert Porterfield's birth, situated just about exactly on the cusp between two very different astrological signs, Sagittarius and Capricorn, makes for interesting speculation to say the least. For a person who seemed, right from the start, to be born for the magic of Theatre, some discussion of one of the magical arts appears more than just appropriate; it seems somehow necessary.

Sagittarians are generally considered optimistic and freedom-loving, jovial and good-humored, honest and straightforward, intellectual and philosophical, but tend also to be almost blindly optimistic, somewhat irresponsible and restless. They are said to be witty and good conversationalists, so they often make good promoters and salespeople. In horse-and-buggy days Sagittarians were widely regarded as unbeatable horse traders. All were traits that Bob Porterfield would demonstrate amply.

Capricorns, on the other hand, are thought to be practical and prudent, ambitious but disciplined, careful and humorous yet reserved. They can often be both pessimistic and fatalistic. They are driven, and they often pursue their own goals at the expense of friendships and family relationships. They can be overly demanding of themselves, their peers, and those who work for them. As one person who knew Bob Porterfield very well, and admired him, admitted, "It was always about Bob Porterfield, always about Barter."

Of course, astrological analogies are easy to make in hindsight. Genetics, upbringing, physical gifts or limitations, and oftentimes just plain luck are certainly easier to quantify. As Julius Caesar put it, according to Shakespeare, "The fault, dear Brutus, is not in our stars, But in ourselves . . . ," a sentiment dear to the hearts of people who do not believe in magic. People who do not believe in magic, however, rarely hear the call of Theatre.

Bob Porterfield's father would not have believed any of this speculation about astrology any more than he would have believed that a sensible and moral person could entertain thoughts of pursuing a career in any species of show business. William B. Porterfield was a no-nonsense man with firm Presbyterian convictions, a great sense of propriety, and a can-do attitude that usually served him well.

He was a handsome man, clean-shaven with large but piercing

eyes that viewed the world from underneath thick eyebrows. He had a long, thin, aristocratic nose, and his mouth formed a tight, almost lipless line with the corners always turned just slightly down.

In his book *The Porterfields*, Frank B. Porterfield (not Bob Porterfield's younger brother, but a distant relative) describes Bob Porterfield's father:

William Breckenridge Porterfield
1875–1944

Prominent citizen, farmer and businessman of Glade Spring, Virginia, was educated at Glade Spring and at Emory & Henry College; was a lifelong member of the Presbyterian Church and was an elder in the Glade Spring Presbyterian Church—was mayor of Saltville, Virginia, for four successive terms; was Secretary and Treasurer of the Smyth County Fair Association; was Secretary-Treasurer of the Abingdon Production Credit Association for more than ten years; had been manager of the Mathieson Farms at Saltville.

In 1909, W. B. Porterfield accepted the position as overseer of some twenty thousand acres of land owned by Mathieson Alkali Works in Saltville, Virginia, only a few miles from his father's farm. He relocated his young family to Saltville, and all that Bob Porterfield was ever able to remember of Austinville was crossing the New River in a small rowboat.

The family's new home was a large farmhouse south of the town of Saltville but with a view of the town about a mile away across a flat, boggy area known as the "well fields," punctuated with springs of salty water where animals had been coming for thousands of years to lick the salty mud and crystalline deposits. Some of the saline-hungry animals, such as the woolly mammoths who visited, ended up mired in the muck and died there, leaving their huge bones to be discovered and still heartily argued over by paleontologists, archaeologists, and their brethren -ologists.

Native Americans also knew the area. Some traveled for many miles to collect salt and to try to bag a mammoth for the tribal larder, all the while trying to avoid being killed and eaten themselves by the local bears or saber-toothed cats. By the time of the War Between the States (or, as some present-day southerners only half-jokingly refer to it, the "War of Northern Aggression"), the salt industry had become well-established and was vitally important to the Confederate armies, because at that time the only practical way to preserve any quantity of meat was by packing it in salt. Naturally, the Union army realized this and sought to put a crimp in the Confederates' salt pipeline, while the Johnny Rebs, also naturally, were determined to keep the bacon moving. The hills surrounding Saltville are still pocked with earthwork "forts" where Rebel soldiers manned batteries of cannon to defend against anticipated invasion by federal troops. It was actually not until late in the war, on October 2, 1864, that the first of two battles for the saltworks occurred. The fighting lasted all day and ended up as more or less a stalemate, although later southern "historians" would revisionistically decree the Blue Coats as "overwhelmingly defeated."

The second Battle of Saltville occurred on December 20, 1864, when a large Union force under the command of General George Stoneman entered the town. It found little resistance because Saltville had by then effectively been starved out by the war. Only a few old men and young boys armed with ancient flintlock muskets and mostly inoperative shotguns showed up to face the unwelcome visitors, but the locals quickly fled or surrendered. The Yanks did not even bother to raze the loot-poor little town but simply marched to the saltworks, broke the salt evaporating kettles they found, busted up the furnaces, and burned down a few buildings.

Some iron salt kettles survived by being overlooked or hidden, and the Confederates were able to produce a little salt in a day or two. By then, though, it was evident that the bid for freedom by the Confederacy had been a disastrous idea. Fewer than four months later, General Robert E. Lee finally concluded that his beloved Virginia had suffered enough and handed over his sword.

By 1909, Mathieson was no longer manufacturing salt, but the raw product of the wells was used to increase the production of alkali, a chemical found in many everyday products from cleaning

compounds and baking soda to industrial fluxes used in steel production. The company was booming.

The Porterfields were quite prosperous by the standards of the
day. Because of William Porterfield's business and political activities, he held his family to a high standard of conduct, fully expecting
that each of his scions would become a respected and prosperous
pillar of his community. "We had, above all," reminisced Bob
Porterfield, "the stern responsibility of upholding our position as
the sons of William Breckenridge Porterfield."

— 1 —

No Turning Back

"Not one of *my* boys is going into that wicked show business!" thundered William Porterfield, shattering the usual tranquility of Sunday morning breakfast.

From the head of his table, Porterfield, dressed as he always was except for the most informal of occasions in coat, stiff-collared shirt, and dark gray tie, leveled his gaze on ten-year-old Bob, his second-to-oldest son, as if he could not believe what he had just heard. A bite of fried ham impaled on his fork seemed frozen in front of him halfway to his mouth, and the drifting steam from a cup of hot coffee at his left elbow was the only thing that moved.

"Yes, sir," confirmed the boy, his eyes locked resolutely but respectfully on those of his father. "I have decided that I want to be an actor, and I am going into the Theatre."

The elder Porterfield shook his head slowly from side to side. "No," he said. "I have high hopes for you, perhaps in the ministry or law, maybe even politics, but as your father I cannot allow you to fritter away your life. Carnivals, minstrel shows, and, God forbid, theater, are no places for any decent young man, especially a Porterfield."

"But, sir . . ."

"Robert. That will be quite enough."

With that, William Porterfield resumed eating his breakfast as calmly as if the incident had never taken place. He was a man used to having his opinions accepted without question and his orders obeyed. For him, the conversation settled the matter.

The boy's eyes dropped to his half-eaten breakfast, but he said nothing. He could sense that his older brother Lilburn sitting across the table from him was itching to laugh but didn't dare. Six-year-old Graham stared at his plate, and his other two brothers, William, age four, and Frank, not quite to his first birthday, happily went on eating as if nothing had happened.

Bob glanced toward the other end of the table to where his mother sat, his eyes searching for her support. Daisy Porterfield was a small woman, solidly attractive with large, dark-brown eyes and hair just beginning to show the first streaks of silver. The faintest flicker of a smile crossed his mother's face the way that sheet lightning sometimes plays around a distant thundercloud at the end of a long hot Virginia day in August.

"We shall see," she said quietly, and the boy knew then that although his father had absolutely forbidden his dream of a theatrical career, he still had a chance. The young Porterfield also realized, even at the age of ten, that his father was both a good and a fair man and that he wanted only the best for his five sons. He later recalled:

> I ought to say right here that my father came from six generations of bluestocking Presbyterians. The Porterfields came to this country before the revolution. My mother's people had lived in Tazewell, Virginia, for at least five generations back, on land bartered from the Indians. My great-grandmother walked five miles to church and back every Sunday. It would have been sinful, by her lights, for even a horse to be worked on the Lord's Day. All my relatives, as far back as I could count, were solid, substantial citizens, pillars of the church and community, lawyers, generals, judges, editors, preachers. None of them, needless to say, had ever entertained thoughts of going into the rash and wicked theatre.
>
> My father's opinion about the theatre wasn't the classic comment of the classically indignant, bigoted father. Because he wasn't. He was a good man, distinguished in a community of distinguished men. I never heard him lose his temper or say an unjust thing; he was one of the best bosses that God ever let live. He had a great deal to do with all our appreciation of what was right and what was wrong. I suppose my declaration came

William B. Porterfield, Bob
Porterfield's father. "No son of
mine is going into that wicked
show business!" he said.

Bob, probably about the age of eleven
or twelve, feeds an orphaned lamb. He
always loved animals of most any sort.

Saltville, Virginia, circa 1912. This is the house in which Bob Porterfield
grew up. The two-story barn uphill from the house is where Bob staged his
first plays at the age of seven. (Photo courtesy of the Museum of the Middle
Appalachians, Saltville, Virginia)

as a genuine shock to him. He must have wondered, somewhere along the way, where in my normal healthy outdoor boyhood, untroubled by poverty or psychiatry, I acquired my burning passion for the theatre.

I don't know either. I knew no actors after whose lives I might pattern my dreams. There were no frustrated thespians among my relatives, though I've often thought that my father, himself, with his towering presence and impressive resonance, could have made a magnificent showman had he so chosen. Certainly no longings such as mine troubled my brothers. I remember L.B., my oldest brother, laughing at me for playing our Victrola, and saying there was more music in a hound's bay than in any musical instrument ever played by a human being. Often, lying in the woods, listening to the bell-mouthed hounds drawing in for a kill, mingling the salvo of bass and tenor and baritone, I was inclined to agree with him. I went on listening to our Victrola, though.

Bob Porterfield, nearly half a century later, painted his boyhood in Saltville, Virginia, as a very special time and place: "The first house that I can remember was the spacious frame house in Saltville. . . . There I was taken when I was scarcely three years old, there I grew up and loved and fought and went to school and acquired most of the ideals and ambition and common sense that have stood me in good stead ever since."

There were two large trees on the front lawn, an oak and an elm, and two grape arbors in a pole-palisaded side yard. A photograph taken of the farm at about the time Robert Porterfield would have been growing up shows at least eleven outbuildings including a pigpen, chicken house, spring house, and, most importantly, a two-story barn in which the young Porterfield, at the age of seven, staged his first plays for cousins. The nearest house appears to be at least a quarter-mile away and there are plenty of open fields, little streams, and patches of brambles.

The boyhood I knew there has since become a vanished way of life. What boy now has a memory of a black Negro mammy [Mary Trueheart], of great vats of homemade apple butter steaming in his mother's back yard, of stolen days playing hooky from his one-room schoolhouse to listen to the bay of hounds hot on the chase? Who remembers now hitching oxen to drag in wood for the gigantic dining room fireplace, or the tune of a good spit on a hot, hot log? Wealthy we were not, though we did have the first dial telephone in the state, thanks to my father's position as mayor [William Porterfield was mayor of Saltville, 1920–24 and 1926–29], and we were among the first to enjoy the luxury of central heating. We scarcely ever saw money; for we raised nearly everything we ate on our own farm, smoked our hams and cured our bacon. Dad gave us all haircuts on Saturday afternoons, with an oatmeal bowl held over our heads.

Though we had servants, the five of us boys had eight or nine cows to milk in the morning before school, and when we got home there were always chores around the house or farm for us to do. We shared in all the work of the farm, and in harvest time, rode up in the wagons and pulled hay down while we felt it move under our feet. We took part in the excitement of hog killing and fought over the bladder and joined in the feasts of hog liver, brain pudding, and sausage that followed.

Our amusements were homemade save for the new Victrola proudly displayed in the parlor and the Saturday treat of a movie. We had horses to ride, as long as we curried them and groomed them ourselves.

His mother had taught him to read before he started school, but Bob's formal education began in Saltville:

My first school was a one-room schoolhouse with a pot-bellied wood stove where about four grades were gathered together. We had a community drinking cup and a lot of other things long since deplored; corporal punishment, for instance. I can still remember the way our principal, Mr. Charles Anderson, would puff up his cheeks and blow through his teeth. "Young man," he would say, "I think you need discipline." And he would proceed to give it to me. Somehow, however, I never thought of my education as being underprivileged or myself abused.

And out of that one-room schoolhouse, what teachers! Even though I was not an especially brilliant scholar, they made me love reading and the world of almanacs, encyclopedias, and poetry. I remember Mrs. Moore; she was beautiful and vital and filled with a zest for living. Her cheeks were rosy, her eyes snapped, and she wore the most beautiful hats I had ever seen. She taught Sunday school as well as grammar school, and I think the enthusiasm with which she taught us Bible stories had a great deal to do with our appreciation of that good book.

I remember Miss Verge Caspry, too, and her Shakespearean quotation bees. They must have been in the eighth grade, and they worked something like a spelling bee. We were divided into teams, and each person had to recite a Shakespearean quotation in turn. If you couldn't remember a quote, or if you re-cited one incorrectly, you had to sit down. The team with the last person left standing, of course, won. I remember late afternoons in the schoolrooms, when the magic of Shakespearean phras-ing mingled with the hot flush of schoolboy competition. Some of my favorite quotes come to me now: "I am Sir Oracle, and when I open my lips let no dog bark." "I am as constant as the Northern star, of whose true-fix'd and resting quality there is no fellow in the firmament." The one I loved best was: "Here shall we sit and let the sound of music creep into our ear, soft stillness and the night become the touches of sweet harmony." We went home afterward and pored over our family volumes of Shake-speare, culling new lines for the next "bee."

The woods and fields around Saltville also held a fascination for the young Porterfield, as it did for most boys of that place and time.

I was not, I hasten to repeat, a model scholar. I learned to love the outdoors better than I loved my books. Every spring a sort of sense came over me of when the first flowers would be blooming on the cliff overhanging our house, and I would clamber up, scrambling among rocks and roots and briars to bring the first blooms down to my mother. Throughout the spring and summer I would luxuriate in the jack-in-the-pulpits and may-apples and hundreds of other blossoms that grew on our meadows and woods. I loved to go out after supper, sit on some mossy log and listen to the dogs' baying and watch the stars come out.

The North Fork of the Holston River, which runs through Saltville, as well as numerous small streams and ponds nearby, gave up stringers of trout, red-eyes (rock bass), and huge white suckers with their silvery white, almost translucent bellies. Giant bullfrogs were plentiful for the gigging, and in the early spring an enterprising boy could quickly fill a gunny sack with horny-heads, a tasty variety of large stone-roller minnows named for the prominent bumps that develop on the heads of spawning males. It was the rare home indeed that was without an arsenal of rifles and shotguns in those days. Every boy—and not a few girls—learned early in life how to shoot and handle firearms safely. Hunting and trapping were accepted facts of life, and wild game such as rabbits, squirrels, quail, and grouse were frequent entrées on nearly every table, those of both the well-off and poor alike.

One of my favorite occupations was raccoon hunting. Inadvertently, 'coon hunting taught me a highly successful method of playing hooky from my books. I had been treeing what I thought was a 'coon. It turned out to be a skunk, with results easily predictable to myself and my clothing. Now I knew, as all country boys know, that if you bury clothes which have been sprayed by a skunk, within a few days all the smell will have been absorbed by Mother Earth. But I hung my mackinaw in the woodhouse for the time being, and a few days later put it on without thinking. It was cold that day in the schoolhouse, and as I leaned up against the pot-bellied stove, an unmistakable aroma began to fill the room. Within a short while class work was impossible. Sternly, the teacher demanded, "Robert, go home!"

After that, whenever I wanted the freedom of the woods for a day, I would get out my old mackinaw, sprinkle a little water on it, and wear it to school. It was four or five such holidays later that my mother and my teacher put their heads together and confiscated my coat.

Even Saltville, tucked far away back in the hills of Southwest Virginia, could not avoid being wrenched into the modern world as the United States began to assume the role of a superpower. The First World War, euphemistically called the Great War, began in 1914 and made America realize that it could no longer function in blindered isolation. Bob Porterfield was only nine years old on June 28, 1914, when Archduke Franz Ferdinand, heir apparent to the Austro-Hungarian throne, was assassinated at Sarajevo by a Serbian nationalist, the act that unleashed the already simmering war, but even young Bob was affected, if only in a small way.

> World War I came during my first years in the one-room school-house. My world was not greatly changed by it. We learned that we had to clean our plates for the sakes of the starving Armenians. We used molasses instead of sugar. I noticed soldiers and girls walking through the woods and hills, hand in hand and arm in arm, because the government had built, near our place, a factory that made gas from a substance of the air known as argon. I knew that the great walnut trees on our farm had been given to what my father called The Cause. We children were set to gathering walnuts, to be charcoaled and made into gas masks.
>
> I was aware of mothers and fathers reading the casualty lists, but, boy-like, the strongest memory I have of the war is that of selling Liberty Bonds. The drive was at full force, patriotism raged strong in those days, and I was exulting in the newfound discovery of my flair for salesmanship. Everyone in the county soon knew that I was selling bonds, and all my father's friends through the bank bought theirs from me. By the time the war was over I had sold more bonds than anyone else in the state. I even got a special citation from President Woodrow Wilson. It was almost as exciting as being allowed to hitch up the oxen and share in the man's work of bringing young saplings down from the mountain to be cut up for firewood.
>
> Of Armistice Day [November 11, 1918] in the mountains I do have a vivid memory. When the news arrived at our house, all of our family and all the servants and neighbors gathered on the top of a hill that overlooked the countryside. My father lifted an old shotgun to his shoulder and shot it into the air, and then the minister knelt upon the ground under an oak tree with the fall leaves blowing in his face and began to pray. He prayed for a lasting

peace on earth, and asked for our country to realize its responsibility to God, to Christianity, and to the world by taking a firm hand
in the making of peace. There were a few songs and tears, and
then we boys ran, laughing and shouting in glee, down the hill
and off to bed. The Great War made me aware, vaguely and for
the first time, that hate and fear existed in the world.

Bob Porterfield was almost thirteen years old, that mysterious period
in a boy's life when both body and mind begin undergoing drastic
changes. It is a time when a boy's desires and those of his parents
often conflict. William B. Porterfield had every intention that his
second son with his obvious gifts for oratory and salesmanship
would become a minister, but the younger Porterfield stubbornly
clung to his dream of a career in show business. It was not just a
dream for him; it was the only dream.

"The boy I look back on now was a boy's boy," Bob recalled,

mischievous and full of fun, as ready as any of his brothers to
sneak off on a coon hunt or join in a corn cob battle with the
neighboring boys from Smokey Row. Yet I knew that I was different, I had found another world. How, I knew not. A realm very
different from my brothers', which satisfied the hunger of my
imagination and decked my pants with spangles. I had discovered the Theatre.

Professional theatre was a thing to which the young Porterfield could
not have been exposed, except for, if one wishes to use the term
very loosely, a traveling minstrel show or skits at a carnival or circus. Still, as hard as it might be to envision today, amateur and
what might even be labeled semiprofessional theatre flourished
throughout the isolated Appalachian Mountains of the early twentieth century.

Primitive phonographs were in existence at that time but were
rare, and the selection of programs to play on them was small. Television was still just a dream, although the concept was known and
lawyers already had patent battles well under way. The first commercial radio station between Knoxville, Tennessee, and Roanoke,
Virginia, WOPI, would not broadcast until June 15, 1929. The call
letters, the station's owners optimistically insisted, stood for "Watch

Our Popularity Increase." Even reading, for most people who could read at all, was limited to local newspapers, the Bible, and John Bunyan's *Pilgrim's Progress*. If the people of Southwest Virginia wanted entertainment, they had to invent it themselves, and invent it they did.

Traditional music provided the lion's share of entertainment. Fiddles, banjos, guitars, and mountain dulcimers were the most favored instruments, but more prosperous homes often boasted a parlor piano; a few even contained a foot-operated pump organ. Dances, often held in barns, were popular, as were play-parties associated with corn shuckings, apple butter making, and other occasions.

Churches also provided much entertainment, although neither ministers nor congregation would have ever labeled it so. Long services, fiery sermons, and impassioned singing were the norm, with revivals, all-day preaching, weddings, funerals, and creek baptizings thrown in for good measure.

Appalachian entertainment, however, especially that of a century ago, was frequently of a decidedly more formal and sophisticated nature. As Bob related, schoolchildren were often encouraged to learn lines from Shakespeare, and most also learned to recite poems by such authors as Longfellow and Tennyson. The local newspapers featured many accounts of music recitals, book discussion groups, amateur drama productions, and visiting lecturers with "magic lanterns" who regaled listeners with tales of travel and adventure. Debates were especially popular, often pitting local lawyers and ministers against one another in usually friendly competition. The topics chosen for debate were usually serious, but not always. For example, one debate written up in the *Smyth County* (Marion, Virginia) *News* begged the question: "Should old bachelors pay extra tax to support old maids?"

Against this backdrop Bob Porterfield's first attempt at acting and staging theatrical productions began very early in his life.

> Almost as early as my memories of Mary Trueheart and playing house with my beloved dog Fan underneath the kitchen stove are my memories of the theatre I had created upstairs in the hay barn. I could not have been more than seven years old when I made my discovery that five bales of hay make a highly satis-

factory proscenium arch, and that an old horse blanket will serve as a curtain. Why I should have found this a desirable and necessary end I have no idea. I think it must be that the need to create theatre is one of the deepest-rooted instincts of the human being.

At any rate, I learned early in that barn the keen delight of improvising, sometimes alone, sometimes along with whatever brothers, cousins, and playmates I could coerce into joining me, stories woven from my own imagining and re-created from the books I had read and pictures I had seen. It nourished the fertile development of an imagination that even in the midst of chores and play kept after me and after me for expression. I discovered the joy of leaving myself outside, of becoming a character and taking on, each in turn, the identity of a major-general, a tramp, a carpenter, and a prince. Perhaps even before I knew what an actor was called, I knew I had found my métier.

None of Bob's four brothers ever joined him in any aspect of the theatre. L.B. held several jobs during his lifetime, but he is remembered most as an accomplished horseman. William ended up working in the New York sulfur industry, Graham had a long career with the company that today manufactures Snapper lawnmowers, and Frank, the youngest, became a career Virginia state trooper.

The only relative whom Bob Porterfield could possibly count as being in show business was a first cousin of his mother's, Pat LaVolo, who Bob later claimed was once the world's champion slack-rope walker. Walking the slack rope is considered far more difficult than negotiating the better-known tightrope. LaVolo had started out life as Pat Huffard, and he was destined for a career in medicine. But the Barnes Brothers Circus came to town one day when he was home from medical school for his father's funeral, and despite the somber reason for his visit home he somehow heard the Big Top's siren call. When the circus loaded up its ponies and elephant and moved on, Pat left with it and he never looked back. Believing that an Italian-sounding name fit the world of canvas and sawdust better than his real one, Pat changed his last name to LaVolo. He and his wife, Wilna, known as Willie, and their three children were later star performers as "The Five Willies" with the Cole Brothers–Clyde

Beatty Circus. During World War II they had a contract to tour with a traveling USO company performing for Allied troops all over the world.

> I had heard about Pat at that time, but I had never met him. In fact, I had never met any actor, nor had I ever seen a play on stage. I had gone to the movies on Saturdays in those days when a child could go to the movies for a nickel, and I had looked forward all year long to the arrival of the Chautauqua tent, the high spot of every year. Add to that the rowdy minstrel shows of the county fair, with the stolen delights of the hoochie-coochie dance, and you have the sum total of our family's experience of the living stage. What little I did know about the theatre I must have culled from an occasional copy of *Billboard* that came my way.

What Bob felt about the theatre he had learned from his dreams and daydreams. Drawing upon his scant knowledge of what the great theatres of Broadway must be like, he envisioned the Great White Way, David Belasco, Walter Hampden, and hundreds of the other personalities of the theatre that he would someday know in person.

Bob never attempted to rationalize those visions and others like them, dreamed long before he had ever smelled grease paint or thought about attending the American Academy of Dramatic Arts in New York City. He believed all of his life that he had a psychic streak, perhaps bequeathed to him through his Cherokee heritage. Soundless symphonies would sometimes creep up on him when he was walking in the woods far beyond the reach of radio, phonograph, or musical instruments. He claimed that a dozen times or more, dreams of running cattle warned him of impending death and disaster; at least once, a dream helped him find important missing documents. Three times, he believed, an eerie psychic instinct saved him from almost certain death. And in his dreams his passion for magic and grandeur found its dwelling place in the world of the Theatre.

His mother understood and supported her son's aspirations even if his father did not. Bob loved her dearly and always claimed to be her favorite child, that he held a special place in her heart. Perhaps it was because he scrambled over the hills and rocks to bring her the first blossoms of spring, perhaps because he appreciated and admired her hats, or perhaps because he was unashamed to show his affection for her. "She always cherished me," he said, "giving me the place of the daughter she had always wanted and never had." She stood by him and encouraged his enthusiasms, helping him make costumes, learn his lines, and gather props, backyard scenery, and even audiences. She became one of the strongest supporters an apprentice producer could have ever wanted.

There were teachers who also encouraged his ambitions. A few might have spotted a gleam of genius, but more likely they recognized his bullheaded determination to make a career in the Theatre even though most of them had no more knowledge than did he about what such a career required or if it was even possible. In any case, they did their best. As it turned out, Bob's catalyst for his first full-fledged acting role was his high school Latin teacher, Miss Eleanor Jennings.

The class was deep into Julius Caesar's *Commentaries on the Gaelic Wars*, and inevitably Shakespeare's *Julius Caesar* was chosen as collateral reading. Bob could never recall if the idea was his or that of Miss Jennings, but he remembered desperately wanting to play the character of Brutus. Egged on by young Porterfield, the class agreed that staging the play would be great fun. The only problem was that Miss Jennings insisted the drama be translated and then presented entirely in Latin.

For weeks the class laboriously transliterated Shakespeare's iambic pentameters into second-year Latin. The students painstakingly memorized their lines, and an assembly day was scheduled for them to give their play to the entire school. Props were gathered, scenery scrounged from all over Saltville, and bed sheets, counterpanes, and towels folded into togas and tunics. The proud day arrived at last, and draped in his mother's finest linen tablecloth, Bob Porterfield climbed onto the podium to begin the famous "Friends, Romans, Countrymen" speech.

"*Tacitu, Romani,*" he announced loudly in southern-accented Latin. "*Ubique sit sulentu!*"

His classmates and the rest of the school immediately burst into wild applause.

It was at that exact moment that Robert Huffard Porterfield made his most important discovery about the Theatre. He discovered the sheer joy of using an audience's enthusiasm to boost his own. Right then and in many plays to follow, Bob admitted that whenever he was out in front of an audience he soared beyond himself and began having a wonderful time. The laughter, tears, suspense, and applause of playgoers gave him a reckless abandon and a near-spiritual inspiration. He knew he loved it.

There was no turning back.

— 2 —

An Actor's Life for Me!

"I don't think it's frivolous to say that I went into the theatre for fun," Bob Porterfield reminisced many years later.

> I had not heard of Stanislavsky then, so I did not know how fashionable and artistic it was for an actor to take himself terribly seriously. I don't know that it would have made much difference to me if I had. I find nothing more depressing than an actor who takes himself without a grain of salt.
>
> Did you ever see a play where the actors got muscle-bound and intense and concentrated so hard on "Art" that they stopped having fun altogether?
>
> If you don't have any fun, Lord knows the audience won't. In fact, if you don't have fun I think you have mistaken your vocation and had better go back to the hardware store or the college drama department or wherever it was you came from.

Bob did have fun and admitted that he became a full-fledged "ham," originally a somewhat humorous derivation of the word "amateur" and describing an actor whose performance is excessively theatrical and overplayed. Whether creating dramas for his own enthusiastic appreciation in the hayloft or declaiming oratory for his classmates or his mother's chapter of the United Daughters of the Confederacy, he knew deep in his heart that he had found his element. He became, in his own words, the "impresario who could make a pageant out of drunken chickens in the backyard and was the costume committee for a fancy-dress version of *The Rival of Kitty*." Every role whetted his appetite for more, and he joined the school debating society just for the chance to talk in front of audiences.

He became the sparkplug that instigated class plays at Saltville High School, and not coincidentally he was usually the leading actor. He was William Sylvanus Baxter, Esq. in Booth Tarkington's *Seventeen*, a humorous novel that recalls the events of one summer in the life of seventeen-year-old Willie. Willie develops a crush on Lola Pratt, a flirtatious visitor to the Baxter household, causing him to experiences the roller coaster–like ups and downs of a self-absorbed and love-struck teenager.

Even though the Theatre filled most of Bob's mind, there was still ample room for the myriad other things demanding the attention of boys. He loved horses and won a ribbon for riding at the county fair. He played with frogs and claimed later to have gotten warts from it. He admits to running away once — at least until supper-time — and he launched many expeditions to dig for dinosaurs or buried treasure. And, when he was twelve years old, he fell in love. Her name was Mary.

> My first love, not really a puppy love, was for a girl with a complexion like ivory, hair as black as soot and eyes big as chestnuts and shining like coals of fire. Mary stood erect like her ancestors; she was half Indian and her father was Irish. It was a wonderful combination, blending in her captivating personality Irish wit and the instinct of the Indians. I would wait at the corner of the road to carry her books to school, and each morning she never failed me. On Sunday I waited for her to go to Sunday school. We talked about our future and our love, our family and our fortune, and the things we were going to do to make the world a little better place in which to live. If it had been the fashion to marry at twelve, I am sure we would have, for we were deeply and devotedly in love.
>
> One spring morning, with the scent of lilacs in the air and a bunch of daffodils in my hand, I waited at the corner of the road for Mary. She did not appear. The first Sunday school bell rang and she had not appeared—the second bell rang and still she did not come, and I, who have never been late for anything, ran so I wouldn't miss the roll call in Sunday school. I noticed when

people passed they would ask if I wanted a ride and I would say, "No, I am waiting for Mary," and the faces of several people fell as they went along.

Finally, when I arrived at Sunday school the teacher met me at the door. She took me into the corner and said, "Have you heard?" Instinctively I knew something was wrong and I said, "Mary didn't come. What is the matter?"

"Mary passed on last night," she said, completely unaware in her own kind way of the blow she was dealing me. "She died in her sleep. Come on now, or we will be late starting Sunday school."

I went into the class and sat in my regular seat. I heard the service, I heard the songs—I heard but I didn't hear, because all the time I was cursing God in my heart for taking away what I considered the loveliest of all flowers in the world, my Mary. During the service I crushed the flowers in my hand to pulp, and when the time came to leave, I went out with a few buds still in my hand, unable to go home.

The brokenhearted young Porterfield didn't go home. Instead he headed for the familiar hills and mountains, a pattern he would continue throughout his life. He walked alone all day and far into the night. When he did go home at last, his mother was waiting up for him. She, of course, had heard about what had happened, and she knew its impact, understanding soul that she was. She had hot milk toast waiting for her son in his room. He ate it without tasting it, then fell onto his pillow and cried himself to sleep.

The following day he somehow managed to go to school but found that his class was being dismissed because of Mary's death. His teacher took him to visit Mary's mother, and knowing of their close friendship, she asked him which of Mary's possessions he wanted. "Nothing," he said, his eyes red from crying, but then:

I saw a little gold heart that had always hung from her neck, and I asked if I might have it. They asked me then if I wanted to see her and I said, "No! No!" I wanted my memory, even then, to be of Mary with a smile on her face and her hair blowing in the wind, and books across her shoulder until she handed them to me to carry. It was the first great sorrow of my life. School was

never the same, and church activities took on a sad note for
many months. The years finally took Mary out of my mind, but
never out of my heart; I have her locket still.

Time and the many activities of a growing boy did eventually let
Mary's memory slip into the curtains, but she never really left the
stage of his memory entirely. Bob moved on with his life, became a
member of Saltville's first Boy Scout troop, and for four years
played first-string football for Saltville High School. He later recalled that it was during conversations with the slightly radical
young football coach that he first heard about the theory of evolu-
tion, an idea that his religious upbringing had never broached and
that later resulted in the football coach's firing.

Of all the joys of growing up in the little company town of
Saltville far from the bright lights of big cities, dancing proved to
be one of Bob Porterfield's favorites. He would one day comment
that he felt young people of later generations lacked the capacity
for sheer fun that he and his friends had back then in the early
1920s. There were hardships, of course, and death often came from
diseases that are today almost forgotten, such as whooping cough,
mumps, and tuberculosis; the great influenza pandemic of 1918
and 1919 did not leave Southwest Virginia unscathed; and there
was the dark shadow of World War I, but taken on the whole, those
were happy times for young men and women.

Their pleasures were homemade and seldom bothered by over-
organization. Whenever somebody gave a dance, people of all ages,
but especially the young, came from miles around by horse and
buggy or driving newfangled motor cars. They came to visit and
laugh and sing, to play "Smells" and other popular parlor games,
but, most of all, to roll up the rugs and dance far into the night.

Dancing came so naturally to the young Porterfield that he could
never remember not knowing how. He danced from the time he
could walk, and he loved it. He taught all his brothers how to dance,
even L.B., the oldest, who seemed to be blessed, he said, with two
left feet. In high school, he began to teach his classmates, neighbors,
and even friends from other towns to do such steps as the bunny
hop, waltz, fox trot, and the wild and spirited Charleston.

> I think now that if I had grown up knowing ballet and good music
> and had a chance to see great ballroom dancing, I would have
> been a dancer rather than an actor. I have always had the great-
> est admiration for people who can use their bodies well, not
> only in walking and moving, but also to express love or hate or
> joy or fear. I was to learn later how much they can add in theatre
> to the importance of a dramatic story.

Bob Porterfield even claimed, and apparently with good reason, that dancing once saved his life. During a summer vacation between classes at Saltville High School, he took a job at the Mathieson Chemical plant, pulling hot ashes and cinders from underneath a roaring furnace. It was hellishly hot, backbreaking work, and even though a lithe and athletic youngster, he got so stiff that he became unable to hold the dancing classes he was conducting at night. He knew that either one or the other—the job or the dancing lessons— was going to have to stop. He decided in favor of dancing and turned in his resignation. On what would have been his very next shift, the furnace burst in the room where he would have been working, scalding two people very badly and killing another. There was no doubt in his mind that had he been there he would either have been killed or badly mutilated with burns. Although he prob- ably didn't think about it at the time, he later came to believe that his thin streak of Native American intuition had served him well.

During his junior year in high school, Bob once again fell in love, this time with a slim and very beautiful girl from Marion named Helen Adkins whom he had met at one of the many dances he at- tended. She was a couple of years older, but he was tall, handsome, and quite mature for his age. In addition, he had access to his father's automobile, an uncommon luxury for high school students in those days. Of all her many attributes, however, two stood out in Bob's mind: she wanted to be an actress, and she was actually attending the American Academy of Dramatic Arts in New York City.

Their mutual interests soon drew them very close, and whenever Helen was home, she and Bob were inseparable. Before either re- alized what was happening, and before Bob was even out of high school, they found themselves headed south down the old Lee

Highway, U.S. Highway 11, to the split city of Bristol, Virginia/
Tennessee, in search of a justice of the peace who would marry them.

> About three-quarters of the way down the road I came to my
> senses. I pulled to a stop beside the road. "Honey," I told her,
> "we can't get married. I haven't even got enough money to buy
> you garters for your stockings."
>
> "That's okay," said the practical Helen. "I can roll them."
>
> "If you depend on me, you won't even have any to roll," I
> said. I turned the car around and took her home.

After that, he and Helen saw less of one another, but for the rest of
Bob's life he could never pass that spot on the highway to Bristol
without remembering the girl he almost married.

Bob's senior year in high school came and would have been relatively uneventful had it not been for the state oratorical contest.
Virginians have always been justifiably proud of that Commonwealth's outstanding rhetoricians—equally at home in the walnut-
paneled halls of legislation or justice, speaking to backwoods farmers
from atop a poplar stump, or preaching hell-fire and brimstone
from the pulpit. For high school students of nearly a century ago
with even the slightest bent toward a public career, winning the
state oratorical contest was the Holy Grail.

The assigned topic that year was "The Constitution." William B.
Porterfield helped his son prepare and practice his oration, and
both father and son felt proud of the speech's rolling thunder and
the opportunities it gave the young Porterfield to display the vocal
techniques he had been so carefully developing:

> When the hand of omnipotence first began to unroll the scroll of
> time, and the newborn world rolled on for ages wrapped in the
> impenetrable gloom of endless night, ages came and ages
> went, cycle after cycle measured its almost endless round, but
> still without a beam of light to cherish its barren waste. The earth
> around its orbit rolled. . . .

Bob easily won the contest at Saltville High School and then represented his school in the district contest. He won that and was

appointed to go to the state capital, Richmond, three hundred miles away, to represent all of Southwest Virginia.

It was the first time Bob had ever left the familiar hills and hollows of rural Southwest Virginia, and it was also his first chance to travel farther than Abingdon or Bristol on the railroad. He and his father rode in a Pullman car almost all the way across Virginia from Abingdon to Richmond. That city awed him with its size, its obvious wealth, and its vitality. Streetcars, automobiles, and spiffily dressed young people seemed to be everywhere, the men in flashy suits and some of the women wearing dresses that were more revealing than anything he had ever seen. W. B. Porterfield and Bob lodged with the governor, the honorable E. Lee Trinkle, who was a fellow Southwest Virginian and a friend of Daisy Porterfield. Bob was assigned the Lafayette Room of the Governor's Mansion for his bedroom. The competition itself was a whirlwind affair, and Bob said later he hardly remembered any of it except that he came out in second place. The student who beat him out just happened to be a native son of Richmond. "It was my first taste of the part luck and politics take in so many of life's honors," he said. "But I was a hero, at least to my town and family. My father was proud of me as he had never been before."

But if William B. Porterfield believed that the healthful life of a country boy, the excitement of football games, laughing and very eligible dance partners, and the triumph in Richmond—which could have been the springboard to a successful career in law or the ministry—had killed his son's dream of going on the professional stage, he was dead wrong.

Still, for awhile at least, the elder Porterfield must have felt vindicated in his denunciation of actors and their ilk. Bob went ahead and enrolled as a freshman at Hampden-Sydney, a small all-male Presbyterian college in southeastern Virginia near the little village of Farmville and about sixty miles southwest of Richmond. Founded in 1775, it was a very distinguished school and perhaps a bit more broadminded than the average church-supported college of its day. With a large, wooded campus and beautiful old Federal-style buildings, its emphasis was on nurturing gentility and Christianity and encouraging high scholastic standards. Always the likable and outgoing young man, Bob made many friendships there, some that would last a lifetime. He studied Bible, English, French, and math and actively participated in extracurricular activities, especially those related to public speaking and theatre. Another extracurricular activity that he would later remember as being especially pleasurable was organized visits to the State Normal School for Teachers in nearby Farmville, an all-girls school. There were parties, picnics, and, of course, dances. But, out of what Bob later described as "that whole hazy freshman year," only one incident stood out vividly. He went to the theatre.

The road show company of *Rose Marie* was playing at the Lyric Theatre in Richmond. Bob and several of his friends decided to see it. The Lyric was colossal to his eyes, with two balconies and a gallery, but he was at first sight a bit disappointed in the furnishings and fittings of the aging building. Both seemed a little shopworn and decrepit. Doubtlessly in Bob's dream world he had pictured all theatres as impossibly beautiful temples of loveliness, and he found the reality shocking. But then the house lights went down, the curtain rose, and the lights and music lifted the young Southwest Virginian completely out of himself. He was lost forever.

> I don't think they write musicals like *Rose Marie* anymore. It was fantastic, it was theatrical, and it was Magic. I can hum some of the tunes still. And the dancing! There was an exhibition dancer with a great white ostrich fan that she could spin and float and curl herself up in like a kitten. I went back to Hampden-Sydney with a dream in my heart that had finally found focus. I walked around in that dream for the rest of my two years at college.

Bob often said that he never regretted the two years he spent at Hampden-Sydney. Time spent studying literature, history, and languages—particularly languages—is, he believed, never wasted. But at that restless time in his life he had no time or patience with the slow-paced drudgery so often characteristic of academic life. Helen Adkins had first given him the idea of attending the American Academy of Dramatic Arts, and at Hampden-Sydney his French teacher and academic advisor to the dramatics club, Dr. Herman

Bell, spurred his hopes of breaking out for New York and a try at a stage career.

Bob was well aware that his father still hoped he would become a minister. William B. Porterfield had even gone so far as to confide his aspirations for his son to the dean of the college. More and more Bob began to feel that gentleman's breath tactfully but persistently down his neck.

> He hoped, they all hoped, that I was going to get "The Call." Finally, one day when he was pointing out to me again the beauty of a life dedicated to saving souls, I rose up in desperation. "Sir," I said to the dean, "I am going to be an actor. I would rather entertain souls than save them."

That summer of 1926, fortified with the laurels he had won for his acting in college productions, Bob informed his father that he had to go to New York City to the academy. As expected, W. B. Porterfield's reply was a resounding "No."

Still by that time Bob saw with such great clarity what he had to do and to be that when he left Southwest Virginia in September, ostensibly to begin his third year at Hampden-Sydney, he didn't

Bob and his brothers, circa 1924. (L-r) Frank, Bill, Graham, Bob, L.B.

even bother to enroll for classes. He hung around the campus for four or five days, avoiding the dean, the college president, and even most of his Kappa Alpha fraternity brothers. Then one morning about five he sneaked quietly out of his dormitory, hitchhiked into Farmville, and boarded a train bound east for Petersburg, about fifteen miles south of Richmond.

Before leaving Hampden-Sydney he had submitted his admission application to the American Academy of Dramatic Arts. While awaiting an answer he worked as a soda jerk at Lum's Drugstore in Petersburg to make enough money to survive. At Lum's, an old-fashioned drugstore where sundaes, banana splits, and Coca-Cola in small glasses attracted the town's young people, Bob worked six days a week from 8 a.m. to 1 a.m. the following morning, a seventeen-hour shift.

Somehow he found the time to write his father back home in Salt-ville, telling him that he could stay in college no longer, that he must go to New York. At night, even though his hours for sleeping were few, he often lay awake burning with the agony of his longing. It was only a mercifully short time later that he received a letter from the academy. With trembling hands he tore open the envelope. He had been accepted!

His father's letter, however, was in his mailbox the next day, and in it the elder Porterfield, not in an unkindly way, informed his son that he had two choices: he could either go back to college or come home. Bob refused both options and threw himself into his long hours at the drugstore soda fountain, saving every penny he could for his coming move to New York. Perhaps from overwork, lack of sleep, or probably from sheer frustration he ended up sick and in the office of a Petersburg doctor who ordered the would-be actor to go home. Bob must have felt truly awful, because this time he obeyed.

When he arrived at Twin Oaks, the Porterfield family home-place near Glade Spring to which William B. Porterfield had relo-cated his family, his father immediately drove him to the hospital in Abingdon for examination. While waiting his turn to be seen, Bob overheard his father talking to the diagnostician, Dr. Frank Smith. The elder Porterfield told the doctor that he wanted his son gone over thoroughly and, Bob later recalled, "especially my head. He was sure that I was completely mad!"

Doctor Smith examined his young patient thoroughly as he had been requested, from the bottom of his feet to the top of — and inside of — his head. His verdict was that Bob Porterfield was "as strong as an ox." He informed William Porterfield that he had never examined a healthier specimen and that the boy's ambition was hardly a mad one. "Why don't you let the boy do what he wants?" he asked.

With that, William Porterfield gave his reluctant consent, and Bob's mother gladly added her blessing with what must have surely been a sigh of relief. She also gave him enough of her hoarded savings to enroll at the American Academy. A couple of days later, a small cloth satchel in hand, Bob boarded the train that would take him out of the hills and hollows of Southwest Virginia to answer the siren's call of New York City. But those hills and hollows back home weren't done with Bob Porterfield, nor would they ever be, and deep down inside he surely must have known it. He was out of the mountains, but the mountains would never be out of him.

— 3 —

How Do You Get to Carnegie Hall?

No one in Bob Porterfield's family at that time had ever been, as he described it, "Up North." Even though the date of his departure was a warm and sunny day in October, with the hills and mountains ablaze in autumnal splendor, his mother was apprehensive. She called him back as he was just about to walk out of the front gate. "Robert," she demanded, "you come back here and put on your long underwear. If you're going to go to New York, I don't want you freezing to death."

Always the obedient son—at least as far as his mother was concerned—Bob Porterfield, although just about to take his place in the Great Wide World, went back into the beautiful old brick house, took off his clothes, and dutifully pulled on his long woolen underwear. Just over his heart, with a safety pin, he secured the little packet of money his mother had given him. He was still clutching his bosom somewhat nervously when he arrived the next day at New York's Pennsylvania Station on what he later swore was "the hottest day of the hottest autumn New York City had ever known."

He had been to the movies, of course, and "knew" enough about New York to expect hoards of famous gangsters to be lying in wait, poised to relieve unwary country boys of every last nickel. His mouth agape at the excitement of the bustling station and the hundreds of people rushing in all directions and with the sulfuric smell of coal smoke from the steam locomotives in his nose, he set out to find a telephone booth.

He had never operated a pay telephone before. After carefully reading the full directions, he took down the hand-piece, inserted his nickel, and when the operator came on the line asked for Circle seven, two, six, three, ohh, the telephone number of the American Academy.

"Would you please repeat that?" asked the operator.

"Circle seven, two, six, three, ohh."

"I'm sorry, sir. I didn't understand you."

"Circle seven, two, six, three, ohh. The American Academy of Dramatic Arts."

There were a few moments of silence. Bob, still glancing nervously about the station for robbery-minded hoodlums and his shoes rapidly filling with sweat, had the sinking feeling that something was wrong with the telephone and that he had just lost his nickel. Then the operator came back on the line.

"Just a minute, sir. I'll go get the chief operator." In a few seconds, a different female voice, that of an older lady with a British accent, came on and asked him to repeat his request.

Enunciating as clearly as if he were back at the oratorical contest in Richmond, he slowly repeated his request.

"Sir," said the chief operator plaintively, "is there anybody there with you who can speak English?"

Not knowing what else to do, Bob hung up the receiver and retrieved his nickel from the coin return.

It was only then that for the very first time in his life, Bob admitted, "I found out that I had a southern accent."

Negotiating his way outside the station, he found a taxi and told the driver he wished to be taken to Carnegie Hall. Fortunately, the driver understood him, or at least the words "Carnegie Hall." Carnegie Hall was the Mecca at that time of all things theatrical, and it housed the offices, studios, and practice stages of the American Academy of Dramatic Arts, America's best-known school of theatre.

Bob was ushered into the president's office, where one final entrance test awaited him; he had to give a two-minute audition in front of a committee made up of faculty members. Still perspiring profusely in his long underwear, he stood up and gave a little prepared speech that he had carried with him from Virginia, then waited for the reaction. The instructors nodded to one another, and then one person spoke up.

"Well, Mr. Porterfield," he said, "you are tall, you are quite presentable, you move with ease, and you have a good, trainable voice, but," he added, "not one of us were able to understand a word you said. If you want to become an actor, you have to lose that southern accent and quickly. We want you to promise that you will avoid all your southern friends for a whole year. Can you do that?"

"Yes, sir!" Bob immediately agreed, accenting the words with an exaggerated up-and-down nodding of his head. It suddenly occurred to him that in that fast city he had no friends at all, southern or otherwise. But he was in!

He stepped out of Carnegie Hall onto the broad sidewalk crowded with more human beings than he had ever seen before in one place — all kinds, sizes, colors, and ethnicities of people. He had always been on good terms with the few African Americans he had known in Saltville, but such a mix of people as he saw now both amazed and excited him. On Fifty-seventh Street, hundreds of cars, trucks, and buses rumbled by, pausing for only a few seconds when the traffic signals allowed pedestrians to scurry across the streets to the blare of horns and the angry-sounding shouts of motorists. Somewhere down the street to his left he heard the tinkle of somebody playing ragtime music on a badly out-of-tune piano. Taking a deep breath, Bob tried to absorb all the sensations of the city he had been dreaming about since his grammar school days when he had first seen it in magazine illustrations. In his dreams New York City had been alive with the glow of stage lighting, had sparkled magically and beautifully. Now here he was while skyscrapers that he could never have envisioned even in his imagination or his dreams reached for the sky so far that they seemed to be leaning in toward one another. Looking up made him dizzy.

New York was, indeed, everything he had expected — and nothing like it at all. Somehow he had come to believe that New York would be the same as the small towns he knew, Saltville or Abingdon or Bristol, only glorified, taller, and more glamorous. As he later wrote, "The New York that I came to in 1926 was beautiful all right, in certain slants of light and at certain times of day, but it was the beauty of a glowing cauldron of hustle and bustle, crudity and impersonality, roughness and competition. It was fast-moving and honky-tonk; it set the pace for the rest of the Roaring Twenties."

Bob found a small apartment above a speakeasy from which the sound of music, laughter, and tinkling glasses could be heard twenty-four hours a day. But, as he later remarked, during the Roaring Twenties and Prohibition, living above a speakeasy was nothing unusual; everybody seemed to live above a speakeasy.

For the first few days, the handsome brown-haired country boy smiled and spoke to the strangers he passed, but he grew hoarse before he admitted that no one was greeting him back. It even took a long time for him to realize that he was walking at half the speed of everyone else, the way a heavy log floats down a flooded river while the fast currents swirl around and go past. In the long gray winter months that followed, when dirty snow caked the sidewalks and cold, wet winds howled through the gray concrete canyons, the city when he wandered alone through it began to echo with loneliness. Although he had steeled himself for the world in which he had chosen to be, Bob began to search about him for some link with the stability of his home in Virginia. It had been, in fact, the rocking chair with a pink flowered cover that made him choose his apartment on Eighty-fifth Street and Riverside Drive. It reminded him of his mother and Twin Oaks. Several months would pass before the lanky young Virginian would quicken his pace to match the frantic scurry that symbolizes New York City.

He immersed himself in his lessons, often studying late into the night to make up for his lack of a social life and sometimes awakening slumped at the kitchen table or on the floor, his textbooks lying crumpled beside him where they had fallen.

Bob's two years at the academy turned out to be, as he later described it, "a necessary stage in my development as an actor," but there he developed his belief that the real school of acting is performance before as many audiences and as great a variety of audiences as possible. "All the classrooms and theories in the world," he wrote, "cannot create a talent, but they can kill one." Trying to be too intellectual about the craft of acting, he thought, robs a performance of its heart and soul. But, although he apparently failed

to see it at the time, without his experience at the academy, it is unlikely he would have ever enjoyed the success he did. The academy
not only taught him more than he was willing to admit; it also gave
him invaluable ties with his fellow professionals in the Theatre,
showed him the ropes, and made him at home in his chosen universe.

Along with the techniques and terms of theatre, he was learning
respect for the Theatre as an institution. These experiences were
tempering his raw boyhood enthusiasms into a professional's hard
axe of dedication. A professional, in Bob's mind—whether an actor,
stage technician, or any of the other legions of people it takes to make
live theatre happen—was a well-trained artist, not some sort of carnival drifter living on the often shady edge of society. He believed
from the start that theatre professionals deserved both respect and
appropriate compensation as hard-working members of a fiercely
competitive art form. He rejected the Victorian idea of the actor as
a social outcast, and he also challenged, throughout his life, the idea
of amateur theatre's value as an educational experience, an instrument for self-expression, or, worst of all, a form of therapy. He felt
that theatre professionals should have dignity in the social scale and,
above all, should be able to make a living at the work they love, "for
that," he said, "and that alone, makes a person a professional and
not an amateur."

He absorbed the language of the stage the way dry moss absorbs
rain: the difference between upstage and downstage, how to rig scenery and lighting, how to fly scenery and light battens from a pinrail.
He took classes in pantomime, fencing, body movement, and acting
techniques, such as how to "cheat front" by turning his face three-
quarters toward the audience instead of giving them a full profile.
And he worked relentlessly on losing his southern accent.

Charles Jehlinger was dean of the academy during those days,
an autocrat of a man, aloof and meticulous, and the students thought
of him, although respectfully, as a dictator. He demanded that his
students think of themselves as creative artists and that they should
always give every audience the very best they had in them no matter their physical or emotional condition. Deep down Jehlinger
knew that only a few of the eager young people in his care would
ever become great actors, that great acting is spontaneous and

emotional, but this did not stop him from drilling them as merci-
lessly as any marine sergeant ever drilled recruits. His specialty was
technique, but his passion was character and flow. He taught the
students to keep their eyes open and their heads held high and to
stay in character well past their exit doors. He demanded that comedy have the snap of static electricity on a dry day.

"Just converse. Don't act. Don't anticipate, just listen, listen, listen!" he would loudly repeat over and over, often stomping his feet
for emphasis. "Stay aware, stay sensitive and relaxed, and just let
the play happen to you."

One of his favorite maxims was "Continue thought, theme, and
mood until otherwise interrupted!"

Later in his life Jehlinger became deaf, but he kept directing the
same scenes and plays, repeating the same maxims, reading lips
and relying on instinct to tell if a student was playing honestly and
in character. "You need the understanding of all human nature,
the sense of beauty of the artist and the poet, the sense of rhythm of
the dancer and the musician, the mentality of a philosopher and sci-
entist," he would say. "Acting is the universal art." But he was far
from perfect. He could inspire confidence, but he could just as easily and readily destroy both confidence and youthful enthusiasm.
"Use your God-given intelligence, you idiot!" he would scream at
those who incited his frustration and anger. Fortunately, either
Bob failed to incur his venom or, if he did, Bob was able to let it roll
off his back.

Despite his persisting loneliness, Bob found 1920s New York
City endlessly exciting. When not in classes or studying, he probed
the great metropolis's broad avenues and alleys, always searching
for the glamour and wonders that had so long occupied his fan-
tasies. More often than not he found them. He visited landmarks
such as the aquarium and Grant's tomb and ranging from the zoo
to the Museum of Antiquities. He wore out shoes walking through
art galleries because they were cheap or free; even though he was
receiving a small stipend from home, money was always dear.

Undoubtedly using the good looks and charm that would serve
him so well throughout his life, Bob made friends with one of the
cleaning ladies at Carnegie Hall. She would wink and turn her

head when he would slip up into the gallery of the cavernous auditorium and lie on his stomach between the rows of seats while Toscanini and other greats of the orchestral world rehearsed the symphonies that would thrill the black-tie audiences packing the house that evening. For the budding showman, there was more to be learned and more real drama in the often tense rehearsals than there would ever be in the highly polished performances that the paying concertgoers would hear.

In those years, New York's Times Square, the Great White Way, was accurately called the Broadway of the World, and its stars were internationally known. In 1927, 268 shows opened on Broadway, a record that still stands. Barbara Stanwyck was starring in *Burlesque*, Helen Hayes was in *The Road to Rome*, and Rose McClendon, Frank Wilson, and Evelyn Ellis broke new theatrical ground with *Porgy*, a drama that successfully starred Negro actors in serious dramatic roles in a play meant for primarily white audiences.

A flyer named Charles Lindbergh performed the impossible feat of flying across the Atlantic, and a fledgling movie industry was also taking off in faraway California. Henry Ford produced his 15 millionth Model T. Coast-to-coast radio was on the air, and the newfangled contraption of television was by then being actively tested. Prohibition was ostensibly in effect, but liquor flowed so freely that more than a dozen people in New York City died of alcohol overconsumption on New Year's Eve, 1926. The flush times and gaiety of the Roaring Twenties seemed as if they could go on forever. Only the most pessimistic economists believed that the bubble would ever burst. The bellwether New York Stock Exchange soared past 300 on its way to a record 381.17 on September 3, 1929. Few people in New York City or even in the United States, except for European diplomats, had ever heard of a discontented vagrant and high school dropout named Adolf Hitler who was electrifying ever-larger German audiences with his impassioned speeches expounding his ideas of a master race.

The area in and around Times Square boasted a sparkling galaxy of theatres whose very names were magic to the young Porterfield: Maxine Elliot, National, Henry Miller, Gaiety, Globe, New Amsterdam, and that grand old dame of them all, the Empire. Almost as much as he loved the stars he sometimes saw, Bob loved the decorations and furnishings of the theatres: their crystal chandeliers, the lush red curtains, the replicas of ancient Roman statues, and the gold-gilded carvings of nymphs and satyrs.

Gaining entrance into these famous theatres to actually see shows, however, was anything but easy. Even then ticket prices were astronomical, or so it must have seemed to struggling students. Many of Bob's friends and classmates became experts at what was called "second-acting" plays. They would pick up a ticket stub from the sidewalk at the end of the first intermission and then casually stroll in to claim an unoccupied seat. Since most plays in those days featured three acts or sometimes more, they often saw for nothing the bulk of the performance. Bob said that he knew people who had never seen the first act of a play even though some of them spent several years in New York.

Bob's country-grown pride would never allow him to second-act, and even after he became a well-known theatre professional, he always insisted upon buying his own tickets wherever he traveled. To augment his modest checks from home, he ran errands, walked dogs, and posed for illustrators and artists. With the dollars he managed to earn he bought theatre tickets and fell in love with all the great actresses who were starring that season. Jeanne Eagles, Jane Cowl, Ina Claire, and Alla Nazimova were some of his favorites, but his all-time hero was an actor, Claude Rains. He went to see a play named *Lolly* seven times because it starred Rains, who had become his idol.

Although he is today probably best remembered as the French gendarme in *Casablanca*, Rains was at that time one of the best-known actors on Broadway, and when he finally answered the call of Hollywood, he appeared in more than sixty movies. On the stage, he acted with what Bob described as "utter and complete honesty." Like most successful stage actors in those days, Rains was larger than life, as was acting itself. It was full of grand gestures, rolling elocution, and extravagant costumes. It was also capable of being what would now be called cloyingly sentimental; Eugene O'Neill won the Pulitzer Prize for *Strange Interlude* that year, but *Abie's Irish Rose* set a record as the longest-running play Broadway had ever known.

Yet all of this excitement and glamour could forestall bouts of homesickness only so long. Even though he frequently walked alone through the grassy woods of Central Park, Bob began to miss more and more the mountains, hills, and people that he remembered and loved back home in Southwest Virginia. Deep in his heart he began to admit that someday, somehow he had to find a way of alloying the two loves of his life: his mountains and professional theatre.

Bob had always loved horses and was an excellent rider, but it was a horse that very nearly got him thrown into a New York City jail. On an unusually warm January day he was on his way through Central Park to the academy when he heard the clatter of hooves on a nearby bridle path. Veering off his course to investigate, to his great amazement he spotted an attractive young woman astride a horse he actually recognized. The horse, a mare named Sol Skinner, was the very one that his father had owned and had sold to a stable in New York. Bob was so excited at the sight that he dashed to the bridle path as the horse and rider approached and yelled, "Whoa, Sol Skinner!"

The mare, hearing her name and recognizing a man with whom she had often taken long rambles in the country, stopped abruptly, sending the rider cartwheeling over her head and onto the bridle path. Mortified, Bob rushed to the rider's aid, picking her up, and trying to brush the cinders off her riding habit. He kept attempting to explain that he knew the horse and telling her how sorry he was, but she thought he was deranged or worse and began screaming for a policeman. Fortunately she was not injured, but the more Bob tried to explain himself, the crazier she thought he was and the louder she screamed.

A crowd of gaping onlookers quickly gathered, and Bob realized he was in a spot that was embarrassing or even dangerous. "What stable does this horse come from?" he finally managed to make her understand. "Let's go there, and I can explain everything." The young woman, calming down a bit by then and not wanting to become involved in a Central Park scene, agreed. They got to the stable, and Bob was soon able to explain. The young woman became the first real friend he had in New York, and because she was a Yankee, he could associate with her without breaking the promise he had made to the academy directors about avoiding southerners. Before resuming his way back to classes, he stood in the doorway of the stable and breathed in the good barn smells, the scents of home, hay and harness leather, and, he recalled, "the wonderful pungent aroma of manure."

Bob eventually made other friends, and even in New York City his life expanded beyond the theatre. During his second year there he met a fellow expatriate from Southwest Virginia named Mary Bryant, and to his great delight she loved to dance. The two became dancing partners and enrolled together for ballroom dancing classes at the Roseland Dance Palace. Together they learned to whirl and spin and dip. "I had just gotten to the point where I could hold her over my head with one hand," said Bob, "when my money from home ran out." For Bob to continue with lessons the Dance Palace required an immediate payment of $52.50. "I sat down and wrote out the check on my father's account," he admitted. This was a privilege he was allowed only in the direst emergency.

Long-distance telephone calls were expensive, rare and, in 1926, usually reserved for the most unusual circumstances, but it wasn't long before Bob found himself on the receiving end of one.

"What was this money for?" William B. Porterfield demanded.

"Dancing lessons," Bob replied.

Through the silence on the line, Bob could feel the icy-cold breath of six generations of Puritan ancestors in his father's voice. Obviously W. B. Porterfield did not consider continuation of dancing lessons a dire emergency. "That is the last money you will ever see from me," he stated.

He kept his word. From that moment forward Bob had to pay out of his own pocket for such things as dancing lessons, scarlet hose, and spangled pants. Or do without.

> My father had determined, in his own mind, that I was disgracing the Porterfield name. It piqued my pride. I decided angrily that I would change my name. Robert Porter, perhaps, or Argyle Porter. I wondered how they would look on a marquee.

He was still mulling over his change of name when a friend of his from back in Virginia sent him a note of introduction to Mrs. Thomas

Whiffen, an actress in *Trelawny of the Wells*. A meeting was arranged backstage following an afternoon performance. Bob was led into her dressing room, where he found a charming little lady with thousands of wrinkles and cold cream on her nose. She had a lovely smile and immediately saw the awe in the young man's face. "Would you like to meet John Drew?" she asked.

John Drew! The very name gave him goose pimples. "I would like to very much," he almost stammered.

"She took me by the hand and led me to his dressing room. He stood up when we went in, ever the gentleman, and she told him I was a young actor who wanted very much to meet him."

Drew was a dapper older gentleman, impeccably dressed even backstage, with a very aristocratic mustache and rimless glasses, a Broadway Star in every sense of the word. "What is your name, young man?" he asked, smiling.

"Robert Porterfield, sir."

Drew looked up at the tall young man in front of him, cocking his head just slightly to favor his good eye. "Robert Porterfield," he said. "Robert Porterfield. Robert Porterfield." He seemed to be swirling the name around inside his mouth like a sip of vintage wine. Finally he patted his guest on the back and said, "That's a good name, my boy. I wish you success."

Before he could catch himself, Bob blurted out, "To hell with my family, then. I'm going to keep it!"

He left the theatre that evening with his head held high and his shoulders erect. He never again considered assuming a stage name.

At the end of his first year at the academy, Bob returned home to spend the summer, his head full of new theories, new heroes, and new horizons. The only thing that he didn't take home from his entire first year of study was the experience of actually performing before an audience. Even at that early stage in his career Bob believed that the only raw material an actor has is his audience. He must learn to use the audience like putty, use it to whet his instincts and be able to sense its ever-changing mood to instantly calibrate and recalibrate his timing.

Remembering the thrill of his high school plays, he was itching to get out in front of an audience, but even if he could have managed to find someone willing to pay him for acting, the American Academy had strict rules, one of which stated that students could not accept a professional job until they had graduated. If he couldn't legally be paid to act in a play, Bob surmised, then he would just have to produce his own. He had no experience in production, of course, but he had seen enough plays by then, had hung around enough theatres, and had seen enough rehearsals to have a pretty good idea of what needed to be done even if he didn't necessarily know how. Throwing himself into his self-appointed task, he chose a play and began pulling together a production and dragging in an audience. To his amazement he found that it all came much easier to him than he had ever imagined. With his enthusiasm, good looks, and natural knack for salesmanship, he had soon corralled a cast of friends and family who had always been more or less sympathetic to his theatrical ambitions. His old girlfriend whom he had almost married in Bristol, Helen Adkins, agreed to act, as did another old sweetheart, Alice Wiley; a girl named Nell Atkins; his cousin Pidney Porterfield; and his younger brother, Bill. Bob played the hero and gave to Bill the role of Bud, the hero's half-wit brother.

The play was Lula Vollmer's *Sun Up*, chosen primarily because it required only mountain accents, gingham and overalls for costumes, and a simple set. All the action happened inside a log cabin, which was easily simulated with a few sawmill slabs and some painted logs on big sheets of cardboard. Bob gathered a few chairs from his family's kitchen and commandeered the household storm door, which had been taken down and put in storage for the summer anyway.

Bob and his little homegrown production toured to several small towns surrounding Glade Spring. These included Lebanon, Damascus, Saltville, and even Marion, the sizeable county seat boasting almost six thousand people. He recalled that the troupe must have given at least ten performances. Pidney Porterfield said that the only one he could remember was in Damascus. Pidney was the driver of an old wooden-sided hay truck, the use of which Bob's cousin had finagled from a farmer, and on that particular trip, said Pidney, the gears had locked up and the only way he could get the sets to Damascus in time for the show was to back the truck nearly twelve miles over narrow and twisty country roads. Bob's fondest memory of the "tour" was the day he fell in love with the little stage in what was then Abingdon's seldom-used Opera House.

Summer seemed to fly by but also to creep. Bob was anxious to get back to his studies in New York, but he found great pleasure in actually putting a show together and making it work. He also enjoyed being in the Virginia hills he loved, so different from the concrete canyons of Manhattan, and he discovered that even though his native hill people might not have the education or sophistication of urbanites, they enjoyed a good play just as much and maybe more.

His second year at the American Academy of Dramatic Arts brought Bob many exciting changes. The "basics," the freshman-level courses, were behind him, and he had proven he could cut it. New teachers, new friends, and increasing opportunities to act began to make up his world. His voice improved, and his diction became both distinct and commanding; he could "reach the back of the house." He polished his fencing skills and learned to move gracefully about the stage, following his blocking to the inch and hitting his spots without ever seeming to think about it. His first role at the academy was in George Bernard Shaw's 1911 comedy, *Fanny's First Play*. He was very excited because it gave him his first-ever opportunity to display a lordly British accent, which he was inordinately proud of having mastered.

The plays were presented to invited audiences in the Empire Theatre on afternoons when nothing else was scheduled. On the first of these afternoons, Bob found himself unexpectedly alone in front of the audience because the actor who was supposed to have made his entrance by then was having trouble with his costume backstage. Never missing a beat, Bob strolled nonchalantly around the set to kill time, first examining a vase of flowers, then turning his attention to a bowl of wax fruit. Forgetting his carefully cultivated accent, he smiled at the audience and said, enunciating carefully, "My, that sho' is purty fruit!" The audience howled, and that was, forever, the end of his experimentation with accents.

He was beginning to make the contacts that would end up serving him so well throughout his life. Some members of the academy faculty introduced the promising young actor to people they knew in the theatre, and his fellow students introduced him to others.

The glittering world of Broadway beckoned, so much so that he sometimes went for a day or more without thinking of Virginia, but not often. The final few weeks before his graduation seemed to creep by like cold sorghum molasses but at last, in May 1928, he graduated from the academy. He recalled that with the ink barely dry on his diploma he strode down Broadway with his shoulders back and his head held theatrically high, fully expecting to have his pick of all the parts Alfred Lunt, one of Broadway's most sought-after leading men, had turned down that season.

Although he would not have believed it at the time, he did what few actors have ever done; he landed a part and opened in a play on Broadway the very day after he left the academy. The show was A. A. Milne's *The Ivory Door* that was already several months into a successful run. Another young man, whose single duty in the play was to carry Henry Hull's train, had left the show because of sheer boredom. William Keeley, the stage manager for *The Ivory Door*, had seen Bob in *Fanny's First Play* and called him to come over for an audition—an audition that consisted of Bob trying on the costume and the shoes to see if he fit. He did, and the part was his.

4

The Bottom Falls Out

Bob Porterfield had no lines in *The Ivory Door*, but he did have a costume that fit and that he later, with tongue no doubt fixed firmly in cheek, called "marvelous." It consisted of purple tights, a pink jacket, and a little pink hat perched jauntily on his head. Bob had never seen Henry Hull, who starred as the king, and of course Hull had never seen him. There was no need for rehearsal because Bob's only job was to carry in the king's train, arrange it properly on the right side of his throne, and then stand rigidly with his arms folded, his elbows extended, and his mouth shut. On the first night of his employment he picked up the vermin-infested train of rabbit skins dyed to vaguely resemble ermine, followed Hull in, and carefully assumed his position, his face a dutiful blank. But when Hull, not having been informed that the original train boy had been replaced, mounted the plywood throne and turned to deliver his first line to the audience, he saw a strange person standing beside him. He did a double-take and then addressed Bob out of the corner of his mouth: "Where in the hell did you get those pretty legs?"

Unlike the actor whose position he had taken, Bob never lost interest. "I have never been bored on the stage, and I hope I never will be," he often told people. Instead, he discovered there was plenty to learn from standing rigidly at attention for thirty-five minutes while the actors, technicians, and all the other theatre personnel went about their tasks. He quickly learned how to count the house, but more importantly he became aware of how to listen to the sounds an audience makes. He discovered the truth of the maxim that every audience and every performance is different. He observed positive

audiences and negative ones, with some being both. When an audience arrives at the theatre eager to enjoy a play and is delighted to
suspend disbelief in exchange for entertainment, both audience and
actors enter a wonderful environment of magic and fantasy that
only live theatre can produce. But on the other hand, Bob observed,
sometimes a single audience member who doesn't want to be entertained, who defies the playwright's and the actors' efforts to enchant,
can sour the mood of everyone present. The real troupers, Bob
concluded, are the actors who can quickly feel out an audience's
mood, desires, and expectations and then play upon them much as
a cellist can feel the constantly changing personality of his highly
sensitive instrument as it reacts to atmospheric pressure, moisture
in the air, and even the musician's own emotions. The show really
lives, Bob came to know, when actors and audience meld.

His next Broadway role was a speaking one, consisting of one
line in, of all things, Yiddish, which is probably about as far from
the lingua franca of Southwest Virginia as is possible. The Yiddish
Art Theatre on Twenty-eighth and Broadway was casting for a
play called *Jew Suss*, so Bob somewhat naively went down to read
for a role. He strode into the office and asked the lady there if he
could apply for a part.

"I'm sorry, young man," she told him politely, "but the play is in
Yiddish."

"Oh, that doesn't make any difference," he replied proudly. "I am
a graduate of the American Academy of Dramatic Arts. I can act in
any language!" His idealism or perhaps his appearance of conceit
must have impressed the stage manager, who scratched his chin
and said, "There is a one-line part you might be able to play. Would
that interest you?"

Of course the part interested him. He believed then, as he did
throughout his life, that an actor ought to attempt any role that
tickles his fancy, that allowing oneself to always be typecast might
provide steady work but that it put one in a ditch, albeit sometimes
a lucrative one.

The line of Yiddish, when translated, meant roughly, "Hang the
Jews!" Bob repeated it after the stage manager several times until
he thought he had it memorized accurately. The stage manager told

him to stand by until he could round up Maurice Schwartz, who was the leading man and the play's producer. When Schwartz came in, Bob had been instructed to jump up and shout out the line. While he waited, Bob continued to mumble it under his breath, trying to get his tongue and throat around the strange mixture of consonants and vowels.

Maurice Schwartz was one of the Yiddish theatre's star performers, strikingly handsome with piercing black eyes. He electrified any room he entered. In a few seconds he strode in. The stage manager nodded at Bob, who leaped to his feet and exclaimed his line. To Bob's dismay Schwartz nearly doubled over laughing. Finally, wiping tears of laughter from his eyes, Schwartz told Bob, "That's the first time I ever heard Yiddish spoken with a southern accent." He gave Bob the part.

The young actor learned much from the Yiddish theatre, perhaps most important of all that classic venue's deep respect for its audience. Working with such great theatrical families as the Goldbergs and the Alders and with people such as Maurice Schwartz and Anna Appel, he learned how to project his voice to the balcony rail and how to use makeup. He secretly thought they used too much, but he appreciated that heavy makeup was part of their effort to play to the last person in the last row in the balcony. Bob later wrote: "In every line of their plays I learned to sense the rhythm of playing, the real vitality, the joy and the music that went into every performance. They didn't sing; the show sang."

At the American Academy his instructors had told him never to speak too loudly, never to raise an eyebrow and never to overemphasize for fear someone might take him for a ham, but the Yiddish theatre had no use for introversion and subtlety. What it had and had in spades was vitality, enthusiasm, make-believe, showmanship, and all the rest. In other words, the Yiddish theatre, ironically, had plenty of good old ham. The audiences loved it. They felt that the theatre and the actors belonged to them in a unique and very special way. Bob would use this lesson well.

For many if not most young actors, the first few years are lean and hard, full of closed doors, trudges on foot from one audition hall to the next, and accepting the dirtiest and lowest-paid odd jobs just to eat, but Bob had hit Broadway at precisely the right time.

> I seemed to have escaped those years. I had stumbled over the threshold of the stage in a year when it was brimming with bounty. The theatre was in its heyday. Lavish productions abounded. Belasco and his imitators were in their element. Money seemed to be no obstacle, and any number of tall and presentable young men were needed for set decoration if for nothing else. Radio was in its infancy; NBC had been incorporated in 1926, CBS came in 1927, and already they were demanding more and more trained voices.

Of course, even Broadway in the Roaring Twenties had its flops. Bob said he remembered one play with Ralph Bellamy that opened on Friday evening and closed after the Saturday performance, but it didn't seem to matter. Parts seemed to fall into his lap. In one play he was assistant stage manager and played thirteen different roles. In another, a historical drama involving the great writer Sherwood Anderson, he actually landed the part because of his ability at hog calling.

> After my first Broadway show I had gone home for a visit. It occurred to me to ask Sherwood Anderson, who had retired to Marion, where he was editing two local weekly papers (one Democratic, the other Republican) if he would give me a letter of introduction to anyone he knew in New York. I didn't know him, but I had never been intimidated by greatness, and I knew he knew Horace Liverwright, who was producing *The Dagger and the Rose*. Mr. Anderson gave me the letter, and when I got back to New York I called up Mr. Liverwright and he gave me an appointment. His first question startled me. "Can you sing?" he asked.
>
> I have a good strong baritone and had been studying voice, thanks to a scholarship from the United Daughters of the Confederacy. I took it to help give my speaking voice resonance and range, and I think it did. However, musicianship had never been a strong point of mine, especially since my brother hit me

over the head with my ukulele, and, in those days, a person who sang on stage was expected to know *how* to sing. I said no. "However," I added, "I can call hogs."

"All right. Call a hog for me."

I r'ared back and called a hog with such enthusiasm that it must have curdled the blood of pedestrians up and down Broadway for blocks away. "Very well," said Horace Liverwright. "That will do." I was dismissed from the interview.

I didn't know it then, but in the rudely competitive business of theatre, in the wearying round from office to office and audition to audition, an actor's toughest job is to find some way of making himself memorable, of standing out from the throngs of actors making the same rounds. Evidently, I had hit it. A week later he called me and asked if I could rush out to Atlantic City. He had fired the page who was playing a one-line part, and needed someone to step in immediately. Unwittingly, I had achieved the feat of being in the right place at the right time (the way most parts seem to be cast) and again, I fit the costumes.

Of course measurements could also work against him. A few months later, Bob had landed a part in a production being staged by Clare Tree Major who was quite famous as a writer, actor, and producer of children's shows. Her productions featured very expensive and lavish costumes that were used over and over in many different incarnations. Bob had actually been in rehearsals for almost a week before Major came around to inquiring what size of shoe he wore. Bob told her. "I'm sorry," she said apologetically. "I can't use you. Your feet are too big."

In *The Dagger and the Rose* in Atlantic City, however, Bob did fit into the pink tights and the plumed hat, and his role seemed simple enough. The play was about Benvenuto Cellini, an Italian goldsmith and sculptor, and was set in sixteenth-century Florence during the Italian Renaissance. Bob's assignment was to burst onto the stage in the second act and say his single line: "Have you seen Cellini?" The first act went well, but in the second Bob heard his cue, ran onto the stage, and shouted out his line. To his chagrin the audience roared with laughter. Actors who had never lost their composure on stage suddenly turned away from the audience to hide their faces. Two actors, doubled up laughing, missed their entrances. Somebody giggled out loud from the wings. There was a long and to Bob an embarrassing pause before the show was able to continue. He had no idea what he had done that was so funny and, besides, the play was not a comedy. It was not until after the final curtain that he was told that under the excitement of his first English-speaking line on the professional stage, he had forgotten his carefully practiced American Academy of Dramatic Arts nonaccent and had blurted out in his thickest Southwest Virginia drawl, "Have y'all seen Cellini?" The play turned out to be a turkey anyway, but Bob never quite got over thinking his bungled line had something to do with the play's being canceled the following week.

> I gave up my new accent after that. I can't really blame my relapse on the American Academy. My voice teacher patiently erased all my southernisms, and I practiced hard and diligently. I learned to speak Harvard English and even turn on Cockney or an Irish brogue, but none of this did me much good professionally. Again and again I was cast in parts where my richest asset was my drawl, and I began to spend more time in radio work where my southern accent was constantly on tap. Even to this day, put a microphone in front of me and my drawl gets so thick I can't understand myself half the time.

Radio was growing by leaps and bounds as thousands and thousands of ever-cheaper and more receptive radio receivers found their way into the homes of Americans. The radio broadcasting stations were also growing more powerful, with a few soon able to beam their signal across much of the country. Clear-channel stations, some just across the border in Mexico, boasting transmission towers hundreds of feet tall, cranked out as much as 500,000 watts, with a few stations experimenting with wattage as high as 750,000. Radio, along with the now-talking movies, offered entertainment that was more accessible than live theatre at a much lower cost, and once the set had been purchased, aside from battery replacement in some models or a few pennies worth of electricity, radio was free. Bob, like many actors of the 1920s and '30s, found that radio work was both steady and lucrative. He was soon in at least two daytime soap operas nearly every week, and his parts were not just walk-ons. He was constantly busy, and now he had money to attend plays as often as he liked. Little did he know that everything was about to come crashing down, not just on himself but on all live theatre.

> I was constantly busy. Rehearsing and making rounds, shoptalk and radio filled up my days. I took little notice of the world events that were beginning to crowd around me. I remember the night I went to the opening of a new comedy called *Button, Button*. I laughed and applauded and did not know that the end of the world I had always known had just begun. How could I know? I had no stocks and bonds, and I had just crowned my cup of glory as a rising young actor; I had met David Belasco.

Belasco was getting ready to stage *Mima*, a lavish dramatization of the book, *The Red Mill.* He needed plenty of muscular and healthy-looking young men to be the guards of hell. Bob found himself cast in a small role, but during the weeks of rehearsal he learned more, he later claimed, than he had absorbed during his entire two years at the Academy, or, for that matter, during any two years of his life. "Working with him was a rare privilege," said Bob of Belasco. "He was a master showman."

Belasco always wore his collar backwards, an affectation he had acquired when as a youth he had played the role of a priest, and throughout the rest of his life he seemed to picture himself as sort of a priest to his actors and actresses. His hair was snow white in the 1920s, and he wore it curled into a cascade of little ringlets. He was usually quiet, but when he did allow his temper to flare he could shake the rafters. He kept tight reins on his actors and especially his actresses in both their professional and private lives. He strongly discouraged both the men and women from being recognized in public, insisting that they limit their trips "outside" and that they take such precautions as wearing wigs and sunglasses. "What the public buys is what they don't know about you," he often stated. "And therein lives the magic of the theatre. They want you to be glamorous, to be set apart, to live briefly in a blaze of glory before the footlights and then vanish in mystery."

Bob believed Belasco's requirements for his people were sound showmanship, but that it created many hardships, especially for the actresses. While employed as an actor by Belasco, Bob recalled, he "took a liking to" a particular young lady who was one of the producer's special protégées. Though it was strictly against Belasco's rules, Bob was visiting in her apartment, and the two were talking happily when there was the familiar sound of Belasco's footsteps coming down the hallway. Then the doorbell rang. Bob jumped up, knowing that his presence could very well lead to both his and his friend's being fired. He took a fast glance around the apartment and crammed himself into a dumbwaiter. There, so cramped that he could hardly breathe, Bob waited out Belasco's visit, which was purely professional and completely innocent. All Belasco wanted to do was visit and encourage his favorite. Bob was so frightened that when Belasco departed and the young lady gave him the all-clear, he crawled out, somehow managed to restore circulation to his legs and arms, and then ran. He never again visited in the apartment of one of Belasco's actresses.

Since this was such a formative time in Bob's life and because he learned so much, both good and bad, from David Belasco and because what he learned was to play such a role in his later life, it is well worth the time to let Bob Porterfield reflect upon Belasco's style and influence.

> He created magical theatre in his heyday. He cast and directed and produced his shows with an open hand and a golden wand, and I never knew him hampered by the lack of money. Everything that he did, he did with a flourish. We happened to be in rehearsal over the Thanksgiving holiday while I was working in *Mima*, and he called out and ordered a magnificent Thanksgiving dinner to be set up and served on stage for all of us, complete with several enormous turkeys, cranberries, pumpkin pies, and all the trimmings.
>
> In American theatre, Belasco was the daddy of everything that could make the magic of theatre richer, more glamorous, and more perfect. He introduced spotlights and front balcony lighting. More than any other American producer, he introduced the use of type casting. In the old days of repertory theatre and

touring stock companies, a theatrical company ordinarily consisted of about eight players. There was a young lady, called an ingénue or soubrette; and a young man, the juvenile. There was the leading man and the leading woman, the character man and the character woman, and usually a second woman and a second man, called the "heavy" or the villain. These eight players could, and did, play all the roles required by any play which they performed, with occasional doubling and once in a while drafting the carpenter to play a bit part. The leading man might be a count in a sophisticated drawing-room comedy one week, a spy in a melodrama the next, and a hobo the week after that. He was better at some roles than others, naturally, but the audience accepted the convention of his weekly appearance as readily as it ever accepted the convention of the soliloquy, the aside, or the invisible fourth wall.

Belasco changed all that. If the script of a play he was doing called for a panhandler in the second act, he was liable to go out on the street and bring in a panhandler. He was a stickler for realism and spared no expense or effort to bring it to the Broadway stage. When actors ate meals in a Belasco production you could be sure they were eating a real and complete meal, down to the last olive, and when the script called for them to drink orange pekoe tea, you could be sure that they were drinking real orange pekoe tea, and not colored water. He had a passion for the literal and had created a minor sensation in 1912 by putting an exact duplicate of Childs Restaurant on stage. When it came to creating a setting for *The Red Mill*, our set designer evolved glowing designs for an intricately fitting, magnificently hellish cauldron, completely fashioned of genuine, glowing metal, a miracle of intricacy. A whole squad of carpenters were set to work constructing it, and the time came, the night before dress rehearsal, for all the pieces to fall into place.

They didn't. Somehow—perhaps because the set designer had been an alcoholic and his mind was ever so slightly off-center—everything came up a little short of the mark. One piece was five-eighths of an inch off, another piece three quarters of an inch. Nothing went together.

Belasco never said a word. He ordered another complete set remade—a month's task—and quietly went back into rehearsal with us for another four weeks. I was granted permission to sit just behind him during the rehearsal period whenever I wasn't used on stage. This happened to be most of the running time of the play, because my chief duties consisted of opening the show with a march down the aisle into the orchestra pit and up eight steps to the stage and crossing out of the play by proscenium left. The rest of the time I was free to study and observe, and I made the most of it. I was enormously impressed, time and again, by the great knowledge of lighting, timing, movement, pacing, and direction that he seemed to have at his fingertips.

Despite learning how Belasco worked, Bob retained his preference for the earlier repertory type of acting company, which he always believed provided the best training ground for young actors.

One day Bob got to see how Belasco could play upon the emotions of his actresses, sometimes in a rather sadistic manner. The script called for one of the women — Bob's friend of the dumbwaiter incident, in fact — to play a very emotional crying scene. The problem was this woman seemed completely incapable of crying on cue. Belasco tried to cajole her, he pleaded, he shouted, but she still could not cry. Finally, he stood up, pulled a large pocket watch out of his vest pocket, and looked at it. "I have wasted more than an hour on you!" he shouted. Angrily he flung the watch across the stage, and it shattered into thousands of pieces. He burst into tears. "That was my mother's watch," he sobbed, scrambling on all fours across the stage trying to find all the pieces. "She gave it to me when I was a boy." His body and sweat-soaked silver ringlets trembled, and his voice trailed off in choking sobs.

By now the actress, terrified and heartbroken, was also weeping uncontrollably. "That's it!" Belasco shouted triumphantly as he slipped back out into the auditorium, resumed his seat, and whispered to Bob, "That was an eighty-nine-cent watch. I sent out for it just now." Whether or not she ever found out the truth, forever afterward that actress could produce buckets of tears at a second's notice.

Of course, absolutely nobody escaped Belasco, not even Bob. The night of the dress rehearsal finally came. This time the scenery all fit, and it was a typical dress rehearsal full of frenzy and confusion—and very, very expensive because all of the stagehands were drawing union scale, some at double- or triple-time. There were also about a hundred important invited guests in the audience. Bob set everything in motion as he confidently marched down the center aisle wearing a sixty-pound costume of patent leather and silver studs and, he always claimed, the first zipper ever used in a costume on Broadway. In one hand he held a colorful banner that matched his costume, and in the other glittering silver spangles much like the pom-poms used by cheerleaders. He couldn't see his feet because of the costume, but he had counted the steps up to the stage many times during rehearsals and now strode confidently upward, only to find that he had somehow overcounted the steps or that they had been shortened. He sprawled flat on his face, legs kicking in the air, and the banner and spangles flew in every direction.

Belasco screamed "Stop!" as he lunged from his seat and bounded down the aisle, took hold of the orchestra pit rail, and proceeded to curse Bob at the top of his voice for at least five minutes. "He called me every kind of name I had heard before," said Bob, "and a good many that I hadn't. I had heard sailors, farmers, and my grandfather curse, but never have I heard the language David Belasco let roll at me." When it was over and Bob managed to climb up off the stage, a fellow actor whispered, "You sure caught hell, didn't you?"

Bob nodded in agreement, but he had a foolish grin on his face.

"What the devil are you smiling for?" demanded his comrade.

"I must have something," Bob said, his expression becoming thoughtful. "Otherwise Mr. Belasco wouldn't have taken that much time with me during dress rehearsal."

He was right. Later that evening Belasco came up to Bob, slipped a quarter into his hand, and said, "Forgive me for my little scene. But you know I like to act, too. When people do things like you did, falling down, it gives me an opportunity to act to my heart's content. You come and sit back of me for the rest of the rehearsal."

Bob kept the quarter for good luck all of his life, and when times were difficult or he experienced self-doubts, he would sometimes take the quarter out of its hiding place and look at it for inspiration.

Before he left New York, he got to watch Belasco direct another show, this one a play called *Blind Windows* in which Bob was the understudy for a then-comparatively unknown actor named Clark Gable. The star of the show was supposed to have been Beth Merrill, another one of Belasco's favored actresses whom he was determined to develop into a star of Broadway. During the final dress rehearsal before the play's out-of-town opening in Philadelphia, however, Gable proved what a powerful actor he was to become. Gable, Bob, and the others were portraying convicts on a labor gang, complete with striped costumes. The script called for Gable to grab a sledgehammer and attack one of the guards, and he did it with such realism that his deadly intent actually made the hairs on his own neck bristle. The guard and everybody else on stage, including Bob, suddenly panicked, having no doubt that Gable had indeed gone berserk and was really going to murder the guard and then the rest of the cast. Everyone stampeded off the stage, crashing through the thin plywood walls of the set, diving through windows, and crashing down into the orchestra pit.

Gable was, Bob realized later, one of only a handful of actors who react like electricity to their audience, no matter how small. "We learned that night what millions were to discover later," Bob said, "that Gable was an actor of great strength and virility and realism."

> It was thanks to Clark Gable's gifts, I am inclined to believe, that *Blind Windows* opened and closed in Philadelphia without ever getting to New York. Ostensibly, it starred Beth Merrill, one of the protégés whose career Belasco had fostered and developed. She was good, but Clark Gable was so much better, commanding the scene by his sheer vitality and virility whenever he was on stage with her, that no one could look at anyone else while he was on the set. Rather than have Miss Merrill appear in an unfavorable light, I think, Belasco closed the show without taking it to New York.

Bob was not upset by the closing of *Blind Windows*, but he began to feel in his bones that it was somehow all over, the glamorous Broadway that he had come into at the height of its glory.

> The theatre of the twenties and the very early thirties had been a bonanza, overflowing with money and elaborate fancy and

the roaring high spirits of the Roaring Twenties. It was a sort of plaything of the rich, extravagant in style and mood as well as in settings and costumes. It seemed that there would be a never-ending flow of roles for presentable young men who could wear purple tights and plumed hats well, and none of us had any idea, when the economic collapse of the stock market began to reverberate through empty theatres, that theatre could ever be any other way.

The collapse of its economic structure, however, was thorough and complete. I began to notice, while I was looking for my next job, that shows on Broadway were beginning to have shorter and shorter runs. A Broadway play was still a fanciful extrava-ganza, but there were fewer and fewer of them. More and more actors were competing for the few roles that were still being cast, and, finally, a little later, I began to get downright hungry and take odd jobs. I did not get another role on the Broadway stage for a long time to come. . . . The magical, star-bright Broad-way of my boyhood dreams got lusterless and rundown at the heels. Just as I began to sip of its brimming bounty, the bottom fell out of the cup.

5

This Could Be a Continuing Thing

The Broadway of January, February, and March 1931 was dismal. Thousands of unemployed men and women roamed the gray and icy streets, often ducking into stores or public buildings such as libraries where they tried to warm themselves until a proprietor or librarian began giving them the evil eye. Many of the unemployed were actors or actresses, often gathering in small groups in little coffeehouses where they spent precious nickels for cups of coffee that they nursed until the last sip had become icy cold. Often several friends or acquaintances would move in together and share a shoebox-sized coldwater flat on the thirteenth floor, and there were many rent parties that tried to raise enough money to hold off insistent landlords for another month.

Even before the crash of Wall Street, however, American theatre was, beneath the glitter and glamour, already struggling with a wide gamut of challenges, some internal, some external, and a majority self-inflicted. In her 1970 Ph.D. thesis, "Robert Porterfield's Barter Theatre of Abingdon, Virginia: The State Theatre of Virginia," Anne St. Clair Williams writes:

> While the American national economy was booming during the 1920s, the American theatre was beset by a number of problems. A decline in activity on the road had begun in 1910. At the same time, the theatre was becoming more centralized in New York City, where the number of productions steadily rose until 1926. Theatres were being built rapidly between 1924 and 1928. Beginning with the 1926–27 season, however, theatre activity in New York also began to decline.

> Among the causes often cited for this decline of the theatre
> in general are: the rivalries between theatre owners, managers
> and booking agents, particularly the Shuberts and the syndi-
> cate of Klaw and Erlanger; the decline of the road and the cen-
> tralization of the theatre, the star system, poor productions; and
> the competition of the motion pictures which began to talk in
> 1929. In New York, unionization, rising real estate costs, and
> strict real estate laws designed to prevent fires are also blamed.

The ever-higher production costs could not be covered by increased
ticket prices, especially since people could now be entertained by a
movie with famous stars for a fraction of what a theatre ticket would
cost. Plays thus had to run longer if the initial investment was to be
recovered or a profit turned. Offerings that performed poorly during their first few nights were quickly closed to cut losses. Producers began to cut corners and lower standards, further alienating
potential audiences.

Many theatre owners and producers had taken to investing heav-
ily in the stock market as they desperately tried to make up for their
losses. When the market crashed on October 29, 1929, it took
many of them down with it.

Some theatres, primarily those owned by the Shuberts, began im-
porting foreign productions complete with ready-built sets and full
casts of foreign actors. American actors and other theatre people,
the handful who could find any work at all, agreed to drastic cuts in
salaries. Many of the grand old theatres were converted to show
movies. Theatres and opera houses in large and small towns all over
America were also made into movie theaters to purvey the steadily
increasing stream of motion pictures being reeled out by Hollywood, some of them slapped together in less than a week from start
to finish. Even though the quality of the films was often low, they
were still a novelty for many, and a man could take his entire family
to see a movie for a couple of dollars, possibly even a double-feature
complete with a cartoon such as *Steamboat Willie*. Warner Brothers
had brought out the first "talkie" in 1927, *The Jazz Singer* featuring
Al Jolson, a former Broadway star who had "gone Hollywood." But
it was, ironically, David Belasco who sold Hollywood its first full-
fledged hit, *The Gold Diggers*, for which he held theatrical rights.

That movie was quickly eclipsed at the box office, however, by a dog. Rin Tin Tin made the first of twenty-six movies in 1924.

Many trained and talented actors left New York—and the theatre—forever. A lucky few transitioned to movies, a handful found work of sorts with the Works Progress Administration (WPA) or Civilian Conservation Corps (CCC), many eventually drifted back to wherever they called home, and a few just plain drifted, hoboing south to Florida or west to Texas or California.

Bob Porterfield was luckier than many. At least he had a home and family that he knew would welcome him back to Virginia where, although money was as scarce as it was everywhere else in America, people still knew how to feed themselves on what they could raise, shoot, barter for, or catch. William B. Porterfield was by that time mired in near-ruin financially because of his real estate speculation, but he managed to save from the bankers and creditors the core of the Porterfield family homeplace, Twin Oaks, along with almost a hundred acres of land. Staples such as sugar and coffee still had to be bought with cash, but cows provided plenty of milk, butter, and cheese; both domestic and wild bees made honey for the taking as long as a few stings could be tolerated; the rich valley soil of Twin Oaks produced copious amounts of vegetables and fruit; and those mainstays of Appalachian farmsteads, hogs and chickens, assured the people of ham, eggs, and Sunday dinner. In addition, equipped only with four or five feet of copper tubing, a few pounds of sugar, and some gunnysacks of homegrown corn, many mountaineers knew how to turn their otherwise unsalable crop into a clear, pure, and fiery product for which townsfolk could almost always scrape up a few nickels or dimes. Sometime in March 1931, Bob marshaled his resources for a railroad ticket to Glade Spring, subleased his little apartment in New York, and caught a midnight train pointed south.

Unlike many of his peers, he had little if any intention of abandoning the theatre forever, as reflected by the fact that he kept his apartment in New York, but he realized that he needed a break from the depressing rounds of fewer and fewer auditions, and he also knew that a month or two of his mother's good home cooking would certainly do him no harm.

For a few days he managed to lose himself in farm chores, visiting with old friends, and having long talks with his mother, but it wasn't long before the siren song of theatre had him itching for the stage. Nearby Emory & Henry College, a liberal arts institution founded by the Methodist Church in 1836, allowed Bob to address one of its morning assemblies. Glenn Kiser, who was a sophomore that year, remembered the morning well. Years later he spoke several times to various groups in and around Abingdon about his recollections of what happened. He gathered some of his thoughts into an article published in the winter 1984 edition of the *Emory & Henry College Alumnus* magazine.

> In the spring of 1931, while I was a student at Emory & Henry, a young Broadway actor named Robert Porterfield appeared at our assembly one morning to make a talk. I had never heard of the man, but I soon learned that his family home was only a short distance from our campus, that he was a graduate of the American Academy of Dramatic Arts, and that he already had several good Broadway roles under his belt. Mr. Porterfield told a number of amusing stories about his experiences in theater, and he explained to us that, at the moment, he was "at liberty" (which I learned later was a showbiz euphemism for "out of work and starving to death").
>
> A few days later a notice appeared on the bulletin board announcing that Robert Porterfield was interested in organizing a summer theater in this area and set a date for auditions. I didn't give a thought to making a fool out of myself by reading for a Broadway actor, but members of the college Drama Club kept pestering me to go and I finally gave in. A few days later a notice appeared listing those who would work in the first play. Incredibly, my name was on it. The notice also informed us that the first rehearsal had been set for the following night at the town hall in Abingdon and that cars would pick up the Emory group. The next afternoon two huge, shiny automobiles arrived, one a Cord and the other a Cadillac. Both were driven by women. Bob introduced us to one driver, Mrs. Mildred Lincoln, who had been a musical comedy star on Broadway before marrying John D. Lin-

coln, a Marion (Virginia) furniture manufacturer. The driver of the other car was Miss Janie Wassum, also of Marion, who had majored in drama at some finishing school.

When the would-be thespians arrived at the Abingdon town hall, Bob welcomed all of them and then announced that the play he had chosen for their first production was *Hay Fever*, a new comedy by Noel Coward. The lead role in the play, Judith Bliss, was to be played by Mildred Lincoln; David, the husband, by Raymond Francis (E&H '32); Sorel, the daughter, by Bly Garnand (E&H '33); Simon, the son, by Tommy Hughes (E&H '34); and Clara, the maid, by Judith Miller, the daughter of an E&H professor. Other cast members included Joe Worley (E&H '33), Sandy Tyrell, Janie Wassum, Virginia Huff (E&H '31), and Glenn Kiser.

Then began three weeks of the most concentrated and bone-wearying rehearsal imaginable. Bob was determined to get a professional performance out of us, so seven nights a week we went to the town hall and worked until well in the morning.

We opened at the town hall for a two-night run, and the house was packed for both performances. Better than that was the wonderfully warm reception the play and the cast received. The audience simply would not stop applauding.

Bob insisted on putting the makeup on everyone himself, and for this job he would don an old smock, such as artists wear. This garment had originally been pink, but extensive use had rendered it dirty and mottled with every color of grease paint known. Bob liked the smock and would wear it backstage during the performance. Opening night, after we had taken our third bow and the audience was still applauding, Mildred Lincoln ran into the wings and pulled Bob on stage, smock and all. The applause was deafening, so we used that bit after every performance.

Following the two performances in Abingdon, Bob took the show on the road to Bristol, Emory, Rich Valley, Marion, Wytheville, and even as far as West Jefferson, North Carolina. No record remains of admission prices or even if admission was charged, but every performance saw packed houses and wildly appreciative audiences.

Before they were even finished with the first play, Bob had his troupe rehearsing for what was to be their next billing, *If Four Walls Could Talk*, but, according to Glenn Kiser, Bob received a call from his agent in New York who told him he was needed to audition for a new play being cast. (Kiser stated in his article that the play was *The Petrified Forest*, but it hadn't even been published in 1931, and if Bob landed a part at all in 1931, it was such a small role that no record of it can be found.)

After the reception for his production of *Hay Fever*, Bob must have surely confirmed his belief that there was a market for live theatre in America's hinterlands and specifically in his beloved Southwest Virginia. Even with the American economy falling apart and much of American society apparently tumbling into chaos, inside the mind of Robert H. Porterfield the pieces of a dream were coalescing. Owen Phillips, who later worked with Bob for many years and who became his dear friend and confidant, was convinced that the idea of a permanent summer theatre in Southwest Virginia, more than likely situated in Abingdon, was born in the spring and summer of 1931 and was not the sudden epiphany so cherished by local historians and publicists.

Glenn Kiser often recalled a remark Bob made one night after playing *Hay Fever* to a sold-out crowd.

"This," said Bob, "could be a continuing thing."

6

Rita of Cascia:
Patron Saint of the Impossible

The Broadway to which Bob Porterfield returned was far from being as lighthearted as it tried to appear to the public—and to itself. Orchestras were notably smaller, directors got by with fewer extras, and the theatres grew ever more run down and shabby. Casting calls were far fewer than he remembered, and the lines for them seemed longer and longer.

For the first few years of his career Bob had been luckier than most. Being out of work, which has always been and still is a recurring way of life for most actors, was not something that had truly struck home with him, but now it did. He certainly was not alone, and a far larger percentage of his friends needed work than had it. Even the more established stars of Broadway could now be glimpsed haunting auditions and waiting in breadlines with character actors and bit players. The few shows that actually opened to promising reviews rarely ran for more than two or three months, and those to often half-empty houses. Hollywood seemed to be, if anything, bleaker than New York. Even the one slightly brighter spot, radio, was feverishly converting its format of live shows to one that featured recorded music despite union strikes and court battles to prevent the move.

"A good many of America's 12 million unemployed, it seemed to me," Bob said, "were actors out looking for work. As we watched closing notices posted on theatre after theatre, the chances of things getting any better seemed to be dwindling away altogether."

Radicalism began to sprout throughout the city, with Communist cells forming and a few people even beginning to openly call for the government's overthrow. A handful of actors and playwrights formed the Workers' Laboratory Theatre, close to Union Square, and occupied themselves with writing and acting in impassioned tirades of propaganda such as *Stevedore*, *Steel*, and *The Klein-Ohbach Strike*. The Communist Party started the New Theatre League and attempted with little success to spread its message by offering free scripts to little theatres throughout the country. The effort soon folded because of shoddy quality and the socialist stridency for which few Americans had a taste.

Mainline theatrical people tried to help their fellows by setting up a Stage Relief Committee comprising such outstanding individuals as Brock Pemberton, Arthur Hopkins, John Golden, and several others. A little canteen was operated in the Actors' Chapel, where bread and soup were usually available. At the Little Church around the Corner, traditionally an actors' church under the pastorate of Dr. Randolph Ray, bread, soup, and coffee were sometimes served. At the Union Methodist Church, Selena Royle, Bessie Beatty, and William Sauter established the Actors' Dinner Club. Tickets that could be exchanged for a meal at the club were distributed through various actors' organizations and dispensed to hungry actors, free for those who had no money or at a small price for those who did. To lessen embarrassment for diners, the tickets were printed so that nobody could tell who had been able to pay something for his or her meal and who had not.

Even amidst a situation where formerly wealthy businessmen and stockbrokers resorted to hawking apples on street corners, Bob managed to ferret out enough odd jobs to keep himself fed, although sometimes just barely. He modeled for art students and wielded a mop at the New York Athletic Club for tips. John D. Rockefeller once tipped him a dime, as did New York Mayor Jimmy Walker and Charles Lindbergh. From the mop he was promoted to elevator operator to desk clerk and then transferred into the dining room as its supervisor but where the pay was still barely subsistence level. "That was a miserable year," he said. "I learned more about running a residence and about serving and preparing and handling food than I expected to use in half a dozen lifetimes, and I hated it." Then, just when he began to believe that matters couldn't possibly get any worse, they did.

A few days before Christmas 1931, he came home late one night after closing up the club's dining room to discover that the door of his apartment had been kicked down. Dirty snow had drifted in, and the icy cold apartment had been stripped of everything, including the bedsheets, Bob's pillow, and his single blanket, a moth-eaten army-surplus relic of the First World War. Every stitch of his clothing including his underwear and a small bag of dirty laundry was gone. The thieves had even taken his skillet, sauce pan, plate, and bowl, and a knife and fork he had borrowed. Nothing at all was left but bare walls and the nail where a calendar had hung. Even that was gone. The haul for the thieves didn't amount to much, but for Bob it was everything he had, and there was no money to buy any more. In desperation, at one o'clock in the morning, he went to the apartment of some friends, managed to wake them up by pounding on the door, and then slept on the kitchen linoleum underneath several layers of newspapers with his shoes and folded-up trousers for a pillow. He fell asleep at last, his mood as gray as his covering of newspapers and as bleak as the news printed on them. The next morning he learned from the friends that Walter Hampden, in some desperation himself, was casting for a cross-country tour of *Cyrano de Bergerac*.

Bob went to see Hampden that day. Hampden looked at him understandingly, as if he might have somehow heard of the theft. He gave Bob a small part in the cast that included, of all things, a live horse, and rehearsals began. Bob borrowed a blanket and a couple of sheets so he could sleep in his own apartment on the lumpy cotton mattress—the only thing the thieves had considered not worth stealing. Less than two weeks later the troupe left New York. When it did, Bob finally gave up the apartment because he could not afford to keep it.

If the Great White Way seemed dim and down in the heels in 1931, the theatre scene outside of New York appeared positively dark and getting darker by the day. As Bob's train rumbled west he realized that rural areas were still able to produce food, but nobody had any money to buy it even though the prices for farm produce were lower than anyone could remember. Wheat was going begging at fifty cents a bushel and corn at thirty-one cents, with perishable items such as fruit and vegetables priced even lower but still rotting in the fields. Despite the abundance of food, Bob saw panhandlers and beggars roaming the streets of even the smallest towns. In the lower Midwest and Southwest the situation was even worse because the Dust Bowl, a combination of drought and ruinous agricultural practices, made farming and gardening virtually impossible. Dozens of dusted-out sharecroppers and small farmers with dazed and beaten expressions could be seen heading westward with their entire families and everything they owned in worn-out cars and rickety trucks, and even aboard mule-drawn wagons. From the train windows, Bob witnessed a landscape of ramshackle abandoned homesteads, bank "For Sale" signs, shuttered factories, and dried-up little towns populated by visibly disillusioned people.

> While the breadlines in cities grew longer, the box office lines outside our ticket windows got shorter and shorter. People didn't have the money to spend on theatre tickets, even to see a matinee idol like Walter Hampden in one of the greatest hits of his career. Banks were closing on all sides of us; one closed just in time to swallow up our weekly pay checks before they could be forwarded to another bank. Mine was, I must admit, quite small. I was playing a Cadet of Gascony at the time, and doubling as the Cardinal, and on the nights we played theatres too small to accommodate our horse, I helped Edward Everett Hale III cart Roxanne's carriage into the fourth act. . . . For all this I was getting the minimum road salary, which was not large in 1931. But when it was lost, I was absolutely broke.

That week Walter Hampden paid the expenses of his company out of his own pocket, but by then it was obvious that to continue with the tour would be impossible. The show closed well ahead of schedule, and as the disappointed actors rode glumly eastward in the cheapest seats available, Bob Porterfield's long-simmering desire to take professional theatre to his beloved hills of Virginia finally bubbled over into a radical idea that nobody had tried, at least not for centuries. Contrary to what many have been led to believe, Bob Porterfield's "epiphany" was not an epiphany at all, no sudden blinding light on the road to Damascus. It was just the final coming together of many strands of a dream, a few that were well thought out and others that were based on little more than intuition and faith.

> Some of us were sitting in the club car, heading across the prairies back to Broadway and another fruitless job hunt, when I first found expression for the wild idea that was beginning to form in my mind. The rich-looking fields and grazing cattle and crops piled outside of farm doors seemed to contradict the long lines of people on relief in the cities; nature had been bountiful that season. Save for the dust storms in western Kansas and eastern Colorado, there had been none of the great droughts or floods or pestilence that one usually associates with economic disaster. Prices on farm crops had never been lower. I think it was said that the price of wheat was lower than it had been since the days of Queen Elizabeth I. It was piling up and rotting away, nevertheless, because nobody had any money to buy it with.
>
> To anyone who ever grew up on a farm, or to any boy who ever traded jackknives for marbles, the idea comes naturally to swap for what you can't buy. It occurred to me that WE had something to swap too—culture, entertainment, spiritual nourishment for body nourishment. Why not?

As the black, smoke-belching locomotive rolled eastward across the dark fields and through the depressing little towns of the Midwest, Bob and his fellow actors talked past midnight over his idea. Any kind of positive talk, any idea however wild it might seem, temporarily took their minds off the bleak future awaiting them in New York. Early the next morning, Bob decided to try out his idea on Walter Hampden, who had not been in on the discussions. Hampden followed the tradition of the great actor-managers of his day by keeping himself pretty much aloof from his employees. A devoted family man, he always traveled with his wife, and even though he was ever courteous and genuinely cared for his people's welfare, he was hard to get to know and not easy to approach. But Bob screwed up his courage.

"Mr. Hampden," I said, "People aren't buying tickets because they haven't got the money. Why don't we let them pay for their tickets in farm produce, things we could eat—vegetables, eggs, corn, turkey, ham . . . ?"

I got to the word "ham," and his face fell. It wasn't a very happy choice of words. He was an actor of the old school who had come to stardom through years of touring the English provinces. Perhaps he could still envision vegetables hurled across the footlights. Or perhaps he was just sensitive on the topic of pork, for the popular swashbuckling heroic style of acting had gained him and his contemporaries the reputation as "hams." At any rate he shook his head. With his unfailing courtesy, he told me that my idea, though novel, was completely impractical. Walter Hampden was the first to tell me that my scheme wouldn't work, but he wasn't the last.

New York City was even dirtier and more oppressive, or so it seemed, than it had been a few weeks earlier. Even the few wretched little jobs such as elevator operator or scullery help had dried up. With no job and no room or apartment, Bob counted his blessings when two friends, Claire McCardell and Mildred Boykin, agreed to take him in. Mildred's mother also lived with them in the small flat. Bob and Claire, who later became famous as a dress designer, had some wonderful times together, he recalled. He once even described those days as the happiest year of his life as the four of them coped with the Depression. Once they acquired a bushel of apples and lived on nothing else but apples and water for almost two weeks. Bob juggled his budget to get by on three dollars a week out of the tiny amount of savings he kept secreted in the lining of his coat. He lived on a box of graham crackers and a quart of milk a day, a combination that he had calculated would give him the greatest amount of nourishment for his money. Still, he couldn't help remembering his father's farm, Twin Oaks, back in Glade Spring and the one his father still managed for Mathieson in Saltville.

The Depression had of course slammed rural Virginia as hard as it had hit everywhere else. Banks had locked their doors and would never reopen. Life savings trusted to the banks were gone. Little stores and other small businesses failed by the dozens. The cash

products of Southwest Virginia farmers—mainstays such as tobacco, corn, and pork—went unsold, and farmers cut back their
production to only what they could use themselves or barter with
their neighbors. Auctioneers stayed busy as they cried off foreclosed
farms for a few pennies on the dollar. Beautiful old heirloom silverware and tea sets were sacrificed for a tiny fraction of their value,
and many people buried their valuables such as silverware and china
to keep them out of the hands of foreclosing banks and eviction-
enforcing deputies. The two private schools in Abingdon, Martha
Washington College and the Stonewall Jackson Institute, closed
their doors because they had become luxuries only a few families
could afford for their children. Just as had investors in the New
York stock market, many rural people had also financially over-
extended themselves, usually by investing in real estate, and now
suffered the consequences. If there is anything that Virginians love
as much as their history, it is owning Virginia land. William B.
Porterfield was no exception. "My own father," wrote Bob,

> like so many rural Virginians, had become "land poor," buying
> up property through the wooded hills and cattle pasture of my
> native Washington County. Now, unable to meet the mortgages
> which the banks were calling in, he had to give up everything
> except the home place, abandoning his dream of leaving to
> each of his five sons a farm along with a good education. But
> the family, at least, was eating as well as it had ever eaten before.
> The only food we actually bought anyway was coffee and sugar,
> and after the Depression came we tapped our maple trees and
> used the syrup for sweetening. We had even made our own
> soap at home.

For awhile after returning to New York, Bob patiently stood in
breadlines and frequented soup kitchens, but it wasn't long before
his country upbringing and his pride of being self-sufficient began
to gnaw at him painfully. "I found it awful easy to get used to living
off somebody's donation, particularly if you had the self-righteous
feeling that there wasn't anything you could be doing about it," he
recalled. "I don't know what there was in me that kept me from
staying in the breadline like so many others. Pride, to some extent, of

course, but I think it also had something to do with the fact that the actor's philosophy has always been giving, not getting. And it also must have had something to do with the sense of responsibility I had been brought up to in Virginia."

For much of his boyhood, Bob had lived on the twenty-thousand-acre farm that his father managed, and he grew up thinking of it as the end of the world because when the train reached Saltville it had to turn around and go back. As manager of the farm, W. B. Porterfield and "Miss Daisy," as she was affectionately known, felt a responsibility to not only their farmhands and their families but to others in the town as well. Whenever someone was sick or in trouble, they went to Bob's mother, so in and around Saltville, literally dozens of babies were named Daisy in her honor. When people needed clothes, it was often Porterfield clothes they were given; when a family needed food, it often came off the Porterfield farm. Bob and his brothers grew up with his parents' desire to assist those who needed help or encouragement. Bob couldn't shake off that same sense of responsibility for his fellow actors wearing out their already thin-soled shoes in vain treks up and down Broadway for jobs that simply no longer existed.

As Bob cooled his heels in the offices of producers, directors, the handful of famous actors still able to mount a show, the Stage Relief Committee, the Dramatists' Guild, or Actors' Equity, his sense of being needed often kept him going. His seemingly impossible dream—seemingly impossible to virtually everyone except Bob—was in his mind more urgently than ever. When others told him his dream was insane, and many did, he only kept at it harder than before. To confound his listeners even further, Bob suggested that theatre could not only be traded for butter, eggs, and vegetables, it could be taken into tiny little communities where no kind of professional theatre had ever gone.

> All through the *Cyrano* tour, looking out the train windows, I had become aware that we were taking our drama not to the farmers and the small towns, but to the cities. Being small-town bred my-self (I had never seen a professional play until I was in my fresh-man year in college), I kept wanting to ask, "Why don't we ever

stop at the towns and the rural communities? Why shouldn't they have the niceties of life too?"

Ever since I had fallen in love with the theatre, I had wanted to share it with other people. I didn't like to see the country people—my people—discriminated against. I didn't ask my question, of course; I knew only too well that the answer would be dry and economic. Who could afford to play *Cyrano* for a town with a population of 3,005? I could, I decided.

With what Bob later described as the boldness of youth coupled with not a little madness, he marched into the Algonquin Hotel one afternoon and made his appeal to the Stage Relief Committee. The committee, he said, presented an awesome spectacle to a struggling young actor living on three dollars a week. He couldn't help thinking that any member present could have given him a job. One of these was John Golden, a producer, writer, musician, and one of the wealthiest men in theatre. He could make actors feel that when you walked into his presence, all the world truly was a stage and make you nervously wonder what part he had chosen for you. He was conceited, patronizing, and jealous of his success, but he could on rare occasions be one of the nicest men in the business.

Antoinette Perry was there with Brock Pemberton. Perry was a gracious and attractive blonde, a good director and a first-rate organizer. Pemberton, on the other hand, wore a near-perpetual look of disdain but had a heart of gold. He once told Bob, much later, that to protect himself from his own softheartedness he had deliberately cultivated the reputation of being mean and crotchety. Also there was Jane Cowl, the epitome of a leading lady and looking every bit the queen of the American stage that she was. At that time she was at the height of her success in *Camille*, and with her enormous black eyes and her regal bearing she was, to Bob, one of the most beautiful women he had ever met. Next to her was Rachel Crothers, a seasoned veteran who had turned out a long succession of highly successful comedies. She scared actors with her perfectionism and seemingly bottomless energy. She was very active as well in just about every humanitarian cause in the theatre: the Actors' Fund, the American Theatre Wing, the Stage Relief Committee, and several others.

If this distinguished panel was not enough to strike fear into someone whose latest role had been that of a horse, there was also Arthur Hopkins, one of Broadway's top producers; playwright Austin Strong; and Frank Gilmore, president of Actors' Equity, the union to which all professional actors must belong. Despite this toughest of audiences, Bob swallowed the butterflies trying to swarm up his throat.

> I began by telling them something they all knew—namely that there were a lot of hungry actors walking the streets of New York. There were two kinds of hungering, I told them, hungering in the body and hungering in the soul. I wanted to bring together the actor who was hungry in the stomach and the people I knew best, the people of the Virginia Highlands, because I had a hunch they were hungry for the spiritual nourishment the theatre could bring them. I thought they were hungry enough for it to pay in the vegetables and chickens and jam they couldn't sell.
>
> I intended taking a company of actors to Abingdon, Virginia, I told them, a town of some three thousand population about twenty miles from Saltville, and I intended putting on any plays I could get royalty-free. Our patrons would pay in edible produce, and when the performance was over the actors would go home and eat the box office. The economics were simple, but there would be a little cash involved in transporting the players 603 miles from Times Square and back. If I were to take some of the hungry actors out of their breadlines, I thought it was only fair of the Actors' Stage Relief Committee to provide me with enough money to transport them.
>
> It seemed elementary enough, but those wealthy and successful ladies and gentlemen of the theatre, city bred and sophisticated, looked at me as though I were proposing a voyage to the moon. A few of them asked questions. How did I expect to house a company of players in the Bible Belt of Virginia? Where did I expect to perform our plays? As a matter of fact, where *was* Abingdon, Virginia?

Bob put on his best show of confidence and informed the committee proudly that Abingdon was the oldest incorporated town on the headwaters of the Mississippi River and that it was located in the westernmost end of the Great Valley of Virginia, on the famous Wilderness Road and within sight of the Commonwealth's two highest peaks. He also explained that among the little town's many charms was a town hall, erected in 1830, with a stage upon which many notable actors had performed because Abingdon was conveniently located on the railroad between their big-city engagements in New York and New Orleans. In fact, he continued, that very stage had been trod by the likes of Joseph Jefferson, Sarah Bernhardt, Madam Modjeska, Fay Templeton, Edwin Booth, and even Booth's notorious brother, John Wilkes Booth.

He went on to tell the members of the committee that Abingdon also had the abandoned campus of what had been, before the Depression forced it to fold, the Martha Washington Female Seminary. Bob said that he had already been to Abingdon and arranged permission to present plays in the old opera house, which was now the Town Hall, and that he had finagled sleeping arrangements for free in the Martha Washington's vacant dormitories. Like the wandering troubadours of medieval days who sang and acted for their suppers and places on the hearth by the fireside to sleep, and like the company of players that had visited Hamlet in the remote fastness of Elsinore Castle, Bob insisted, he and his group would be "well-bestowed," sheltered, and fed. "Who knows?" he opined. "Perhaps we might even take in a few pieces of silver." Then he boldly informed the committee that, at season's end and after expenses had been settled, if any of the silver remained, he would share it with the Stage Relief Committee.

> They went into a huddle in the corner while I waited. It seemed to me they took an awfully long time. At length they came, and John Golden was their spokesman. The verdict was *no*. The Stage Relief Committee had no money to supply my actors with transportation to the Highlands of Virginia.
>
> As a group, they turned me down flatly, but, as individuals, they had liked me, in spite of themselves. They seemed to think of me as a sort of lovable lunatic. Perhaps as a tribute to the influence Jane Cowl had among them, perhaps because the whole

idea was all so impractical and unfeasible, and yet stirred their imaginations, they began offering help here and there.

Austin Strong introduced Bob to the Authors' League and helped him write up one of the most unusual arrangements in theatrical history. Bob agreed to pay in royalty one Virginia ham in exchange for the right to produce any play written by a member of the Authors' League to which, at that time, all playwrights for Broadway had to belong. Bob knew that the league's agreement was tongue-in-cheek, but to him it was dead serious. He had every intention of putting on the plays and paying for the privilege. A good smokehouse-cured Virginia ham seemed to Bob fair, convenient, and even poetic compensation because he believed that the writer of the play should also be able to eat his share of the box office take. Strong set the ball into motion by telling Bob he could produce his own popular success, *Three Wise Fools*, even though he knew that, at that time, Bob didn't yet even have a hog, much less a ham, with which to pay his royalty.

Antoinette Perry offered Bob a beautiful silver satin cyclorama she was no longer using, a large cloth stretched tight in an arc around the back of a stage set, often used to depict the sky or simply as a way of highlighting the onstage action. In addition, she and Brock Pemberton arranged for Bob to acquire some used scenery he could take with him to Virginia. Bob also began making the rounds of anyone he knew and many he didn't, getting his foot into as many doors as he possibly could. One of the first people he approached individually was John Golden. Bob figured that even though Golden had turned his idea down in committee, he might be willing to help as a private individual, which is exactly what he told Golden without beating around the bush. Golden had piercing eyes, and he stared at Bob with them for what seemed like hours. Finally, he asked quietly, "Why are you doing this?"

Bob paused, looking out the window of Golden's office to the wintry streets of Manhattan far below, a Manhattan crowded with desperate people out of work, every street corner occupied by at least one of the six thousand men and women trying to sell, for a nickel each, unmarketable surplus apples donated by the International Apple Shippers Association.

"I am an actor," Bob said without turning around, his gaze still lost on the gloomy gray streets below. "I'd rather be doing this than selling apples."

"All right," said Golden. "I'll help you." He gave Bob the right to produce his current hit, *After Tomorrow*, royalty-free.

> They are all dead now, those people to whom I appealed at the Stage Relief Committee that afternoon.
>
> They thought it was impossible. All of them, but one.
>
> I was walking wearily out the door when someone tapped me on the shoulder. It was Jane Cowl. "Young man," she said, "don't let them discourage you. With your youth and your faith and your enthusiasm, I'm sure you can carry it through."

Miss Cowl then reached into her purse and withdrew a tiny lead statue, about an inch high, of Saint Rita of Cascia, the fifteenth-century Italian nun who is the patron saint of impossible causes. According to legend, as Rita was on her deathbed dying of tuberculosis, she expressed a single wish, that she be brought a rose from the garden of her family's ancient farm. Even though it was January, the dead of winter, a friend traveled to her old home, hoping to find perhaps at least a withered flower for her but there in the glistening, ice-glazed snow, she found growing a single bright red rose.

"I want you to take this with you," said Miss Cowl. "And if you ever find somebody who is trying to do something more impossible than what you are trying to do, I want you to pass it on."

Thanking the actress profusely for her encouragement, Bob tucked the little statue of Saint Rita into his threadbare coat as he stepped out onto Broadway into the cold blast of an icy blizzard.

7

"*Rock of Ages*"

Franklin Delano Roosevelt took his first oath of office on March 4, 1933. In his inaugural speech, which contained the famous line, "The only thing we have to fear is fear itself," he addressed many of the issues hovering over a down-but-not-out nation: "The means of exchange are frozen in the currents of trade," he said. "Farmers find no market for their produce." But, he prophesied, "In every dark hour of our national life a leadership of frankness and vigor has met with that understanding and support of the people themselves, which is essential to victory."

Counting on that "understanding and support of the people," Bob Porterfield was ready to begin assembling a troupe of actors willing to test his scheme of a professional theatre based on barter. At the breadline in the Little Church around the Corner where he went from time to time to cook soup and sample a little of the bread and soup himself, Bob saw many out-of-work actors, but to his amazement he discovered that actors out at the elbows were just as skeptical of his idea as the Stage Relief Committee had been.

To actors accustomed to the vitality, however shabby and muted, of New York City and Broadway, the tiny hamlet of Abingdon, Virginia, of which none of them had ever even heard, seemed a remote and lonely place, as alien to most of them as Morocco or Mars. Yes, they admitted, there were indeed a few summer theatres in cities other than Gotham, but those had been around for years in such places as Skowhegan, Maine; Cape Cod, Massachusetts; and Westport, Connecticut—all within a fairly easy day's hitchhike back to the safety of Manhattan. But a professional theatre in the unciv-ilized wilds three hundred miles south of the Mason-Dixon Line was, to them, unimaginable. And did Bob Porterfield actually pro-pose paying them in sweet potatoes and boiled hog ribs? Surely he was kidding. One actress told Bob that she would love to spend a summer in the mountains, but, she asked, in the Bible Belt?

Eventually, however, a few actors began to see the sense — or, at least, the novelty — of Bob's idea, and not all of them were desper-ate beginners. Nell Harrison, a character actress widely known for her gaiety and love of America, agreed to go along, and to also bring her daughter and son-in-law, Eleanor and Charles Powers, who had just closed a show with Ethel Barrymore. Mildred Quiglay, whom Bob had met in the David Belasco production of *Mima*, promised to travel to Abingdon as Bob's leading lady.

Emily Woodruff and Bob Thomsen, who would both be graduat-ing from the American Academy of Dramatic Arts that June, were eager for stage experience however they could get it, even if the pay had to be butchered or peeled before being deposited into their accounts — or bellies.

Arthur Stenning, a fellow member of the aborted *Cyrano* tour, accepted Bob's offer with his typical brisk and cheerful readiness for adventure. He was a British character actor who had fought in the Boer War and mined for diamonds in South Africa before taking the stage in the colonies. Robert Hudson, a white-haired, florid-faced, and courtly gentleman who was presently in *Forsaking All Others* star-ring Tallulah Bankhead, knew that the play would soon close and put him out of work, so he also agreed to throw in his lot with the expedition. Bob wrote the following about his fledgling troupe:

> They were not kids; they were mature men and women of the the-atre, and most of them were older than I was. Some of them were better actors than others, but they were all professionals, and they all needed work. A few days before I left, H. H. McCullum, an elderly character man with a wonderful bass voice, came to me and said he had heard I was offering jobs to hungry actors. He wasn't much of an actor, I knew, but he was awfully hungry. I agreed to bring him along.

Although he didn't realize it at the time, Bob's kindness to the old actor, a kindness that came to him as naturally as his drawl, would soon pay off handsomely in Abingdon.

With a band of actors assembled—smaller than he would have liked—a few trunks full of begged and borrowed costumes, and bits and pieces of stage sets, Bob was now ready to make his move. He went to see Frank Gilmore to confirm the union's agreement to his plan for paying the actors with bartered goods. Whether or not he took Bob seriously, Gilmore seemed glad enough to catch even a faint prospect of actors working and eating, so he and Bob penciled out a short agreement that, Bob later admitted, sounded a little pretentious.

> We, the Undersigned members of the stock company, which is to open a summer season at the Barter Theatre, Abingdon, Virginia, on June 10, 1933, severally acknowledge agreements heretofore entered into with Robert Porterfield, Manager, by which we are at the Barter Inn during the time we shall play, and also a share in the net profits of the Barter Theatre's operations—the share to be thus divided among the company to be at least one-third of such net profits, while the balance of such profits (not more than two-thirds of their total) shall be donated to the Stage Relief and Dramatists Guild funds.
>
> We also acknowledge that individual agreements, embodying a clear and definite understanding as to methods and expenses of our transportation (and including incidental costs en route) from New York to Abingdon, Virginia, and return, have been entered into by each of the undersigned respectively with the above Manager.

If Frank Gilmore knew that the "clear and definite" agreement about transportation expenses primarily involved hitchhiking—and Bob suspected he did—he winked. Bob now had the required union blessings, royalty-free plays, and actors. He had also assembled an impressive list of patrons headed by Jane Cowl and Walter Hampden. All he needed was an audience, and he knew that was up to him although he wouldn't have to do it all alone.

On his trip to Abingdon in the fall of 1932, during which he had obtained the promises of theatre space and lodging for his company, he had also met at an ice cream parlor named Louie's a blue-eyed young woman named Helen Fritz who had been a physical education instructor at the now-closed Martha Washington Female Seminary. With his charm and enthusiasm, Bob easily enlisted Fritz, as everyone knew her, in the cause, and she accompanied him when he returned to New York. In the early spring of 1933, the two of them returned to Abingdon in her car to get one of the school dormitories ready to house the company and to talk up the idea of their theatre.

That is indeed what it quickly became — their theatre. Although Fritz's role in both the theatre and in Bob Porterfield's life was one of willing and enthusiastic helper, few who have given Barter's history serious thought doubt that without Fritz's keen organizational abilities and tightfisted financial management, the theatre likely would not have survived its first season. Bob Porterfield was the creative driving force, the ambassador of culture, and the Gibraltar-like symbol of Barter Theatre, but it was Fritz who asked carpenters requesting four boards to build a set if they couldn't get by with three, who decided if an article of produce was worth a ticket, and who, often quite literally, counted the beans.

On their way to Abingdon, Bob and Fritz stopped in Washington, where they braved a frigid wind off the Potomac River that brought with it a wintry mist to join the throngs of people in town to watch Roosevelt's inauguration. As Bob added his own to the roar of applause that greeted nearly every line of FDR's inaugural speech, he felt a rebirth of hope. It seemed to him, he said, that the morale of the country had taken a sudden upswing, and his own with it. Both the country and Bob's idea were going to be sorely tested in the coming weeks.

He and Fritz arrived in Abingdon the next day, March 5, 1933, which was both a Sunday and the day President Roosevelt declared a four-day bank holiday. The trustees of the Martha Washington Female Seminary for Women had given Bob the use of their gracious white-columned buildings large enough to house two hundred with ease as well as the campus's surrounding estate with beautiful old oaks, golf course, swimming pool, and tennis courts. Every last bed and every stitch of bedding, however, had been removed to Emory & Henry, the Martha Washington's sister institution. All of the china, cutlery, silverware, and cooking utensils had also been hauled off with the exception of one huge cast-iron skillet and a battered old stockpot large enough to prepare twenty gallons of soup. Bob and Fritz found themselves camping on the floor of what amounted to a vast and empty resort hotel, so Bob's first duty as general manager and producer was to go door-to-door in Abingdon begging for unused cots and beds. He quickly wrote all of the actors and actresses he had enlisted to bring their own sheets and a blanket and, he added hopefully, hammers if they had them.

There is no record of how many, if any, hammers actually came, but the actors began arriving early in June. The first to come to Abingdon, on the afternoon train from New York, was Robert Hudson, who had just closed in *Forsaking All Others* in which he had played the Reverend Duncan. According to Bob, Hudson arrived "suffering from his more or less annual bout of the DT's. We put him to bed in one of the downstairs bedrooms, and a small Negro boy was set to look after him."

The majority of Bob's troupe arrived at Abingdon by hitchhiking, and they were, he recalled, "a nice motley crew." Their appearances did nothing to counteract the chilly indifference of Abingdon townspeople:

> Abingdon looked askance at the style of manners and dress affected by actors in New York. Even I, from only twenty miles up the road, knew nobody in town I could call by his first name. I did know plenty of people, however, who looked upon the theatrical profession as the nether limbs of Satan. I knew plenty of people who weren't disposed to take very seriously a band of actors who wore their hair in ducktails. I sat on a lot of front porches, I rocked and I visited, I talked culture to anybody I could get to listen. Most of them seemed bent on ignoring me.

Bob had to admit to himself at least that the Stage Relief Committee had good reasons to doubt his idea of taking live theatre to Abingdon — better reasons, perhaps, than even they realized. Once that Bob was actually in Abingdon, the realization that he had come into a territory where actors were scorned, not idolized, became abundantly clear. Even Bob's father belonged to that great mass of solid Southwest Virginians who regarded actors and their ilk as second-class carnival types, rootless, devoid of morality, sordid, lowly, liable to corrupt children and virgins, and thieving in the bargain. Bob knew that his father and the others could not really be blamed for their attitudes, because the only shows that routinely visited such small places as Saltville and Abingdon were cheap vaudeville or burlesque productions, fifth-rate minstrel acts with performers often just one step ahead of the law, and carnival strip shows presented in small, dirty tents behind the fairground stables.

> Nobody had thought of bringing any other kind of drama anywhere near Saltville, Virginia [and, long before 1933, fast trains and Pullman sleepers had eliminated any need that "name" actors might have had to overnight in Abingdon]. Then, as now, most of the people who prayed for the salvation of the actor's lost soul were the people who have yet to go inside a theatre. My father may not have actually been praying for the rescue of my soul (I think he had too much real humanity for that), but he was a long way from backing up any of my theatrical shenanigans.

Some of the things actors did could be, Bob admitted, a jolt until understood. He related that one day he was in the kitchen of the Martha Washington, informally referred to as the "Barter Inn," when a large African American man named Rufus whom Bob had hired as cook came rushing in, obviously terrified and out of breath. "Mr. Bob, Mr. Bob!" he gasped. "You better come quick! There's a white man out in the yard trying to choke a white woman to death!" The cook had just witnessed his first rehearsal.

Directly across the street from the Barter Inn, the old red brick structure that housed the theatre and stage continued to function as town hall, police headquarters, chambers for the town council, public library, and a dentist's office, which meant that people were always coming and going and poking their noses into rehearsals. In addition, Bob and his actors usually had an audience that could be truly described as "captured," because downstairs, just below the stage, was the local jail. Bob once said he could judge how the plays were going when laughter from below greeted comedies and dead silence prevailed during dramas.

A sort of box office was established at the theatre entrance, and Bob set anyone not otherwise busy to hand-making posters and scattering them throughout the area while at the same time scrounging for props. Everyone also worked hard at building their scenery out of practically nothing and trying to get the Barter Inn habitable. It had a rat's nest of antique wiring and plumbing, and every day seemed to feature a new crisis that sent Bob or Fritz running to fetch their crotchety old repairman and plumber, the only one in town who would venture into the bowels of an old building well-known to be haunted and occupied by such a collection of asylum-worthy Yankees.

Bob and his cook counting up the box office take from the previous night's performance during Barter's first season. Bob and his actors ate well, but never knew from one day to the next just what homegrown food might appear on the menu. Foodstuffs brought in and traded for tickets ranged from cabbages to a cage full of live rattlesnakes. "Them snakes is good eatin'!" proudly proclaimed the mountaineer who brought them in.

An early Barter troupe ready to hit the road.

The actors, many of whom were seasoned Broadway professionals accustomed to star treatment, fell to work with a will. They were proud people, but none complained when assigned to build sets, focus spotlights made out of tomato cans, lay linoleum, or peel potatoes. A few of the men went out to an old falling-down barn where they salvaged boards and straightened out enough rusty nails to build Barter's first set. Whatever the assignment, they must have figured it beat starving in New York City. And it was, after all, a certified—or certifiable—adventure.

They were truly pioneers, those actors and behind-the-scenes workers who ventured into the wilds of Virginia that first year. They were, in alphabetical order: Prentice Abbot, M. H. "Ricky" Austin, Jack Fawcett, Bob Fogle, Helen Fritz, Ruth Guiterman, Nell Harrison, Storrs Haynes, Eric Hellborg, Robert Hudson, Percy Hunt, Agnes Ives, Marjorie Lutz, H. H. McCullum, Hugh Millard, Charles Powers, Eleanor Powers, Mildred Quigley, Munsey Slack, S. Slaughter, Arthur Stenning, Bob Stillman, Robert Thomsen, Chester Travelstead, and Emily Woodruff.

The plays they presented that first summer included: *After Tomorrow, Monkey Hat, Salt Water, Caught Wet, East Lynne, Three Wise Fools,* and *The Bob-Tailed Nag.*

The first production was set for Saturday, June 10, 1933, in Abingdon. For the following week it was set to tour throughout a fifty-mile radius to outlying towns, playing one each night through the following Saturday. In Bob's arrangement with Abingdon for use of the old opera house, he had agreed there would be no performances on Sunday. The initial offering was to be John Golden's *After Tomorrow*, a safe and inoffensive comedy/drama.

Admission was set at thirty-five cents or its equivalent in produce, with children being admitted for a dime or the equivalent. Proudly, Bob and his people put up posters proclaiming, "With vegetables you cannot sell, you can buy a good laugh."

Bob had decided not to act in the opening show. "I was going to greet people," he said,

> sell them their tickets, show them their seats, and then dash back to pull the curtain. I found myself hoping there were going to be people to greet, for I realized on the morning of the day we opened that no one had as yet forked over his thirty-five cents or the equivalent in victuals across the mayor's desk that was now the box office. I suddenly felt the sharp responsibility for the twenty-two people who had followed me in faith all the way from Manhattan. I knew I was right about the actors who were hungry in the stomach; I just hoped I was still right about the Virginia Highlands people who were hungry in the soul. In my pocket I had exactly one dollar. I also had Saint Rita.

Bob and his people did have one thing going for them, and if it might appear to be an intervention by Saint Rita, so be it. On the first Sunday morning that the entire troupe was together in Abingdon, six days before their scheduled opening, Bob issued a call to the actors and then led all of them en masse down Main Street to Sinking Spring Presbyterian Church. Bob recalled that he could feel the coldness around them as they filed into the sanctuary. The troupe took a couple of pews near the back, aware that every eye was on them. "Oh, Lord," someone whispered into Bob's ear. "Why didn't we stay up north where sin don't count?"

The service began with the usual ceremonies, but then the first hymn was announced: "Rock of Ages." As everyone stood to sing,

H. H. McCullum, the old character man whom Bob had allowed to come along primarily because he was hungry, stretched himself to a regal stance and put his whole heart and full rich baritone into the hymn—without a hymnbook.

> *Nothing in my hand I bring,*
> *Simply to the cross I cling,*
> *Naked come to Thee for dress,*
> *Helpless look to Thee for grace. . . .*

Every face in the church turned toward him, but he didn't miss a word even though the organist went through all five stanzas. Out of the corner of his eye, Bob said, he could see icy stares melting into warm smiles of approval. Afterward, people stood at the church doors and invited everyone in twos and threes home with them to Sunday dinner. For many of the theatre people, it was the first good square meal they had eaten in weeks.

That evening Bob sought out McCullum and thanked him for the timely public relations his hymn singing had given them.

"Lord, Bob," McCullum said, shrugging off the compliment. "It's a good thing they picked 'Rock of Ages.' I had to learn it for a part I played a couple of years ago. I hadn't been inside a church in twenty years."

8

Let Her Milk Her Own Ticket!

On Saturday, June 10, 1933, a craggy-faced little farmer—attired in freshly laundered and pressed blue denim overalls, a yellowed-white shirt stiff with homemade wheat-flour starch and buttoned to his Adam's apple, a clumsily knotted paisley necktie, dusty thrice-resoled brogans, and a sweat-stained gray slouch hat—walked through the front door of the Abingdon Opera House, plopped down two fat green cabbages on the mayor's desk, and asked for a ticket to see the show. His name is unknown, and he has long since returned to the good Virginia soil from which both he and his cabbages sprang, but he was the first in a line that would, in time, stretch into the hundreds of thousands and extend to every continent.

"I don't suppose," said Bob,

> at any other time we would have found a community like Abingdon so receptive to our venture. The Depression, in the midst of all the hardship and suffering it created, had nevertheless created the same esprit de corps of poverty in Abingdon that I had found in New York. When everybody was just about as poor as everybody else, there wasn't much sense of snobbery, and there weren't any Joneses to keep up with. There *was* a lot of the milk of human kindness flowing, and people who had suffered had a feeling of responsibility for their neighbors. I daresay in a more prosperous year we would have met with a lot more indifference and a good deal less appreciation. As it was, our jobless predicament and the fact that we were trying a unique way to work ourselves out of it caught at people's imaginations.

The old farmer was quickly followed that day by other farmers, teachers, merchants, tourists, and townspeople. Bob, years later, talked to many of those first-nighters, and few of them remembered much about the play; some of them didn't even remember its name. "What they do remember," he recalled, "is that on that June day in the Highlands of Virginia, in the teeth of improbability, magic began to happen."

By the curtain time of 8:00 p.m. every seat had been sold, every inch of standing room occupied, and people had to be turned away. In the front row sat William B. Porterfield and Daisy, the one beamingly proud of her son and the other reluctantly considering that Bob's wild scheme might just bring pride instead of humiliation to the Porterfield name. The magic continued as the first patrons sat absorbed in the first professional play nearly all of them had ever seen, interrupted only once or twice by the cackle of bartered chickens or the squeal of a small piglet—traded for four tickets—out in the box office. Living, breathing professional theatre had come to the Virginia Highlands.

Actor Bob Thomsen wrote about it to his mother the next day:

> It's Sunday morning and most of the cast is seated around a long table writing letters about last night. It was really swell. I never in all my life had a better time. I guess this is as good a time as any to try to describe the theatre—a large town hall. I learned last night that the last performance given there was over seven years ago. All I have written about Booth's stuff lying around is no exaggeration. It is. But the most exciting part of the place is the fact that the stage is right over the town jail. You can look through a hole in the stage and see the prisoners. I am awfully keen to know what they thought of my performance.
>
> The dressing rooms are right next to their cells, which adds color to say the least. Another outstanding point is that the back stage looks right out on Mrs. Henry's cow pasture—and her animals are not very well trained. At the most dramatic moments in the play they will give forth great resonant moos. I think their favorite actress is Agnes. They never fail to respond to her lines: "I hate you. I hate you!"

Yesterday morning went pretty well. We ran through scenes till about 12 and then came back for lunch. After lunch we sat around here and went through our lines. People started appearing with "barter" about 11 and by the middle of that afternoon the box office was filled with the most amazing lot of stuff it has ever been my pleasure to see. One ticket was bought with a very small baby pig, which has a squeal that can defeat any actor's voice. We put him outside as a barker. We got enough onions to keep us for a century, lettuce, corn, a chocolate cake, and the biggest black rooster I ever saw. It was the strangest sight—stock and vegetables for a ticket. We got to the theatre about seven to find the box office looking like the rear end of Lexington [a wholesale market in New York] out front and people were actually turned away. Several carloads from North Carolina couldn't even obtain standing room. It was wonderful.

Bob and the little sow pig traded for a ticket. Instead of eating her, Bob decided to take her to Twin Oaks, where she became the mother of more than a dozen litters, many of whose hams would end up on the tables of the rich and famous.

Sunday was a holiday for the actors, but on Monday morning Bob Porterfield and his troupe piled the set onto a beat-up old truck named Lizzie and set out for their first date on the road, in Glade Spring some twelve miles away. Because there wasn't any money to buy dinner at a restaurant, the troupe always ate before leaving Abingdon or took a picnic meal with them, and they returned to the Barter Inn every night. Their show was a rousing success wherever it played. Box office action was brisk, and homeward-bound actors often shared their bus with boxes of vegetables, homemade pies, baskets of eggs, chickens, ducks, and other assorted livestock.

The little sow several years later. She lived many years and finally died of old age after doing her bit for the arts.

The local newspapers were very supportive and good about announcing the plays and writing stories on the new theatre, but according to Bob, the first bona fide critical review was written by Sherwood Anderson, the semiretired world-famous author who at that time owned and edited both the Republican *Smyth County News* and *Marion Democrat*. The two papers were located at opposite ends of Marion, and Anderson would work at first one office and then the other, writing the editorials for both. Apparently, Anderson, who later became Bob's close friend, felt the show was above politics because he ran the same review in both papers:

> The play itself wasn't much. It's hard for the legitimate drama to get as bad in plot construction as the average movie, but sometimes it comes close. The acting was much better than the play.

After Tomorrow gave us—and this is really the main thing—an
honest-to-goodness evening in the theatre. And the Barter Theatre will shortly give us more. And so, in preparation for next
Thursday, all good citizens who like to see the drama in the flesh
will accumulate 35 cents in eggs, butter, spinach, strawberry pre-
serves or pennies and wait the next coming of the Barter Theatre.

Bob's crazy idea seemed to be working out. As the good citizens
watched their hens expectantly for eggs or saved up pennies, the
troupe was busily rehearsing and preparing for its next offerings:
Caught Wet, which was a comedy, and *Three Wise Fools* after that. A
sudden sense of optimism seemed to spread like wildfire through
the players, both onstage and off. Nobody worked any less hard
and, if anything, worked harder at rehearsals, painting sets, and all
the other tasks. Perhaps because of the fresh mountain air and the
cool "good for sleeping" nights, or just the fact that they were actually making a living doing what they loved, life for the company
took on a warm and joyous atmosphere. Private enterprise also blos-
somed between other tasks. One actor opened up the college swimming pool to the public for a small fee; another began to teach tap
dancing. The tennis courts stayed in almost constant use, and
bridge games lasted well into the afternoon on the huge white-
columned front veranda of the great antebellum mansion. All of it
was an innocent gaiety, Bob recalled. "The townspeople waited expectantly for a scandal, but we didn't give them one. Drinking was
no problem, for nobody had money to buy liquor, and the occasional jar of homemade 'white lightning' that came across the
counter in exchange for a ticket had twenty-two ways to go. At
night we often piled into the truck and drove out to the Holston
River to swim naked in the moonlight, the girls at one bend of the
river, the men at the next."

Bob and Fritz had decided early on that as a way of bringing in
some much-needed cash, they would rent out rooms in the school's
old dormitories. The Great Depression had created America's
largest-ever itinerant population, as even those who still had a bit
of money drifted somewhat aimlessly about the country either
seeking opportunities or because their lack of stable employment
gave them a sort of dubious sabbatical. Bob decided to appeal espe-

cially to artists of all sorts. He produced a little brochure that offered room and board for ten dollars a week or thirty dollars a month. Without additional cost, he promised, there would be rehearsal rooms for itinerant actors, pianos and practice rooms for musicians, and easels and models for painters; he assured writers also that Southwest Virginia was home to a good stock of interesting mountain folk to study and interview.

A few visitors took up Bob's offer and stayed all summer, but most lingered only a night or two. The nightly room rate was one dollar. One of the people who stayed all summer in 1933 was a Dr. Lapin who took up residence in the basement with several cages of experimental rabbits. Nobody knew or really much cared what he was doing, but his work later became known as the legendary "rabbit test" for pregnancy.

Tales of that first year's box office business have long since become the stuff of legend, and Bob alleged later that most of them were at least partly true:

> There was an old man who came up to the box office with a solemn face one afternoon when I was on duty. "I ain't got no victuals to bring you," he announced.
>
> "Well, what do you do?" I asked. We were glad enough to let people pay for their tickets in professional services. That was the way we got our hair cut and our teeth filled.
>
> "I'm in the underground business." He said it kind of furtively, and I didn't quite know what to make of it. "Underground?" I asked.
>
> "Yep," said the old man. "I make coffins."
>
> "Not this season, thank you, I don't believe we're going to need any." We had gotten into the knack, by then, of believing we might survive. But the old man stood there for a while longer. "I also whittle out walking sticks," he finally said. "If you let me in to see the show, I'll bring you one, and if my old woman comes I'll bring you two."
>
> It was a deal. He came and he brought his old woman, and they liked it so much that before long I had more walking sticks than I knew what to do with. I ended up giving them out among theatrical people in New York, and for a while they were almost

as popular as our Virginia hams. He made them out of roots dug up from trees of sassafras and apple, and they were wonderfully light and strong.

The story that has become my trademark though is about the man with the cow. He came up to the box office window about a half hour before curtain time and asked, using one of the hand-me-down Elizabethan terms so often found among Virginia mountaineers, "How much milk does it cost to get into yer opery?" I did a little mental arithmetic, and I told him it would come to just about a gallon. He nodded gravely, and went back outside. I'd noticed a cow tied to a tree on the Martha Washington lawn, and I watched him take out a pail and milk his cow. Customers came and went, and just before the show started he was back at the ticket window. I had noticed that there was a woman standing over on the lawn leaning against the flank of the cow. "Isn't that your wife?" I asked him.

"Yep," he allowed.

"Don't you think she might like to come see the show too?"

"Yeah, but by God she can milk her own ticket!" The first act was half over before she came in.

On rare occasions, Bob would get a call from an irate citizen whose watermelon patch or apple tree had been raided by young patrons, and one time two little boys showed up with jars of what they said was apple butter. Later the jars were found to contain only red clay mixed with water, but Bob laughed and said that if anyone wanted to see theatre that badly they deserved to get in. For the most part, Bob and Fritz accepted the value of the offering as stated by the would-be patron, and most often the items exceeded the value of a ticket. One time an old mountaineer arrived with a cage full of very agitated live rattlesnakes. "Them snakes is good eatin'!" he proudly informed a very terrified Fritz.

By the end of the 1933 season, according to Barter Theatre's beloved legend, the company had gained collectively 303 pounds and had a cash profit of $4.35, two barrels of jelly, and one sow pig. Bob sent the money to the Stage Relief Committee, shipped the jelly to the New York home for old actors, and kept the pig. It was the same pig that arrived as barter on opening night, but instead of turning her into dinner Bob had dispatched her out to Twin Oaks. In the back of his mind, he said to himself that that little sow pig was going to be the source of his play royalty payments for years to come . . . and she was. In 1934 she gave birth to eight piglets, and in 1935 another eight. A sturdy animal, she remained a patron of Theatre for many years, and in time hams from her lineage graced the tables of such luminaries as Noel Coward, George Kaufman, Phillip Barry, Robert Sherwood, Sidney Howard, Rachel Crothers, Howard Lindsay, and even Clare Boothe Luce. Sometimes playwrights seemed a little skeptical of actually eating a home-cured ham from the wilds of Virginia, but not Fred Allen. He took delivery of his ham with gusto, looked it over carefully, and then asked Bob cheerfully, "Anyone we know?"

When the season was over, the company members found themselves once more out of work and making their ways as best they could back up U.S. Highway 11 to New York City, and Bob was invited to join a midwestern tour of *Journey's End*. No salary was involved, but coverage of his expenses was promised and he was to get a share of the profits if there were any. He left Abingdon in October for Springfield, Illinois, to begin rehearsals.

A 1939 Hirschfeld illustration of the Barter lobby as guests bring in their trades and wait to be issued tickets. Bob is in the foreground.

Because of his experience in Abingdon, Bob was assigned to handle the show's publicity, and to his amazement he found himself setting up shop in an old law office where Abraham Lincoln had once practiced. Bob said that he often wondered what Lincoln would have thought about an actor's presence, knowing that Lincoln had been shot to death by an actor and in a theatre, but also knowing that Lincoln genuinely loved the stage. He walked out to Lincoln's tomb one afternoon and shared his speculations with the aged caretaker there.

The caretaker told him that, early in Lincoln's career and long before anybody outside of Illinois had ever heard of the lanky barrister, a company of players had come to Springfield, preparing to stage a show. A local church congregation, however, was holding a religious revival that same week, and not welcoming the competition, demanded that the sheriff prohibit the play from going on. The actors had no money to feed themselves or even to travel on to the next town, but a young lawyer, Abraham Lincoln, heard about their plight. The case amused him, and, asking no payment, he argued the actors' case before the local magistrate. So eloquent was his defense of their right to perform their art that he won the case.

The tour of *Journey's End* had suspiciously few bookings, and those seemed very haphazard to Bob. The first thing that he noticed, he said, was a sense of leisure after the summer's frantic pace in Abingdon. The company was lodged in an apartment hotel and given credit all over town for meals and the like, even though it was another week before scripts came in the mail and rehearsals began. After two weeks, however, the company arrived in Bloomington, Indiana, and finally enjoyed a full house of cash-paying customers. After the final triumphant curtain, the actors assembled backstage to receive their share of the take, only to discover that the manager had skipped town with the cash.

The actors had all registered at the Graham Hotel in Bloomington and were left with no way of paying their bills. Some members of the company sneaked out of town as quietly as they could, but Bob refused to do so. He went to the hotel's manager and told him that he could either accept a check on his account back in Virginia or that he was willing to stay and wash dishes until the bill was paid.

Bob paused theatrically. "I sure can break a lot of dishes," he said. The hotelier agreed to accept the check.

"The manager of our company was not really a crook," said Bob, "although the FBI later caught up with him for passing bad checks. He was just one of those people of goodwill who seemed to pervade the outskirts of the theatrical profession: dabbling, full of talk and good ideas without the competence to back them up. When he realized he had overreached his abilities in our *Journey's End* tour and made a muddle of it he simply got scared and ran, leaving Bob Thomsen and me hitchhiking back to New York, our pockets and our stomachs empty."

Back in New York Bob discovered that John Wexley, whom he had known as a stage manager in the Yiddish Art Theatre, had become a successful playwright. He had written *They Shall Not Die*, based on the Scottsboro Boys case in which nine African American teenagers, the youngest only twelve years old, had been unjustly charged with raping two white women on March 25, 1931, while hoboing on a freight train from Memphis to Alabama looking for work. Bob's idol Claude Rains was cast in the leading role, and Bob was given a small part, returning him to the ranks of the employed.

He was back working on Broadway in a hit show, a significant new drama that presaged the coming civil rights movement, alongside the star he most admired who was in the most challenging role of his career, yet, oddly, none of this thrilled Bob the way it would have a few years before. His own theatre, in which he had starred and sweated and shook hands and relished the unabashed enjoyment of his audiences, was calling him. At first he tried to shrug off the thoughts, but the sirens of the mountains had powerful voices. As the redbuds and dogwoods burst forth with bloom back in Virginia, Bob had to accept that his heart was really in the hills.

Like any virile young man, Bob chased a few women and had a few chase him. Of the latter, he remembered one in particular. She was older—probably in her fifties—and apparently very wealthy. She had met Bob at a lavish theatre ball, and from then on, she never let him alone. She constantly sent him little notes of endearment and always signed them "The Star of the Sea." She saw his every performance, and one night while he was playing in *Blue Ghosts*, he was handed a note that said "The Star of the Sea is in Box Number 1." He looked out to see her sitting alone in a vast box, surrounded by the theatre's only empty seats. She constantly invited him to come out and live with her on her large estate on Long Island, but he never accepted.

He and Helen Fritz had become increasingly close during 1933. Fritz did not have as much passion for the theatre as did Bob—few people ever did—but she knew the way Bob felt about Theatre in general and his own Barter Theatre in particular. Her drive and her near-fanatical quest for perfection soon made her indispensable. Bob was crazy about Fritz and could not imagine running his theatre without her, but her mother in Bethlehem, Pennsylvania, declared that her daughter was not to return to Abingdon unless she and Bob were married. Fritz and Bob happily agreed that the wedding would take place on May 12, 1934, in the apple orchard of the family's summer home in the Pocono Mountains.

Fritz and Bob planned their whole wedding around the apple blossoms, but a late spring threatened to keep the trees from blooming in time. Undeterred, Bob wrote for advice to U.S. Senator Harry Byrd who was at that time probably Virginia's most famous apple orchardist. Byrd wrote back with the suggestion of pouring boiling water on the ground beneath the trees. So, for the two weeks before their wedding, Bob and Fritz carted barrels of boiling water and poured it on the ground. The morning of their wedding day, with every other tree in the orchard gray and bare, the two chosen trees burst into blossom, cascading pinkish-white petals into the air.

Bob's father had traveled to Pennsylvania to be his son's best man. He had been asked to serve in that capacity, Bob admitted, with an eye toward earning his blessing not only for his marriage to Fritz but his marriage to the theatre as well. The Fritz home was filled to overflowing, so when it came time for Bob and his father to dress in their morning coats, striped trousers, spats, and top hats, the only place they could find to change was in a large outhouse behind a clump of lilacs. When they heard a harp strike up "Lohengrin," they exited the privy into the sunlight and, quite unexpectedly, right into the middle of the guests. The wedding party gave forth with a roar of laughter that Bob and even his determined-to-be-solemn father had to join. The Star of the Sea, whom Bob had invited to the ceremony in expectation of a handsome wedding gift that never materialized, scampered about snapping photographs. A minute or two later, Fritz appeared from behind a little hill on the arm of an uncle, as her father had died of pneumonia when she was still very young. Just then a sudden gust of wind lifted her silk skirts and petticoats high into the air. Her attendants immediately scrambled to pull her dress back down, but Bob noticed all through the ceremony that Fritz kept jerking and twitching. It turned out that a honeybee, attracted to the apple blossoms, was crawling up and down one of her legs, but it finally flew off without stinging, right after Bob and Fritz were pronounced man and wife.

— 9 —

Why Didn't You Wait?

It would be pleasant to say that I returned that summer to Abingdon in triumph with my bride, there to follow up the success story of our first season with new heights of success and mounting days of glory. It would be pleasant, but it would not be true. The second year was the hardest that my theatre ever knew, and it was all we could do to stay put. At one point we came very close to closing altogether. Our box office, with its changing blend of cash and crops, was a sort of barometer of the economic health of the country, and in 1934 the forecast it bespoke was short of rosy. We were too closely tied to the grassroots economy of the soil to retreat to any tower of artistry, and in time of drought we watched the sky as anxiously as any farmer. Not for a moment did we lose our sense of daily crisis; our margin of survival was too thin.

Bob's program of plays for 1934 was far more ambitious than it had been in 1933. Included were *The Late Christopher Bean, Death Takes a Holiday, Coquette,* and *Ten Nights in a Barroom*. Barter's novelty seemed unfortunately to have worn off, and the economy in the Virginia hills had deteriorated even further: farmers could afford neither seeds nor a few pennies worth of gasoline. Only the occasional curiosity seekers or tourists came through the theatre's doors. Performances often played to less than half-full houses, and even those stalwarts who still came seldom had cash with which to pay. Fritz's little tin cash box grew lighter and lighter.

Only the goodwill and generosity of the people of Abingdon and the surrounding countryside kept Barter afloat that year and in the years that followed. Bob's stories of how people and businesses often bent over backward to help him keep his dream alive would fill several books.

He would forever owe a debt of gratitude to many, but especially to the doctors of Abingdon. In the summer of 1935 one of the actresses became very sick and was taken to the hospital. She was there for several weeks, but according to her doctors their tests could not pinpoint what was wrong. Only long after she had recovered sufficiently to leave Abingdon and go home did Bob find out that she had been stricken with polio, and that the doctors had known it all along. They had kept her isolated to prevent the disease from spreading but had conspired to tell no one, not even Bob. They knew that if word leaked of a polio case in the theatre company, Barter's doors would have closed forever.

Another story, a humorous one, involved the sheriff of Washington County. Bob needed a moonshine still for a scene in a play called *Mountain Ivy*, so he contacted the sheriff and asked if he and his men might use their knowledge of such things to help Barter's set designer construct a stage replica. "Hell, I'm no artist!" the sheriff informed Bob. "Why don't I just send my boys out and get you a real one?"

Moonshining was one Virginia industry that prospered despite — or because of — the Depression, so it wasn't hard to locate an operating still. The deputies simply checked around at local stores, found out who had recently bought suspiciously large amounts of sugar, and shortly thereafter brought some ol' boy's operation to an abrupt if only temporary halt. Just as a precaution the sheriff had several large holes chopped in the cooker with axes before handing the contraption over to Bob, lest some of Barter's company be tempted to start producing liquid entertainment with a bit more kick than Shakespeare.

The year 1934 seemed to conjure up one crisis after another. To meet expenses, Bob had to sell his photographic equipment. Whenever the company played out of town, everyone held their breath until enough cash was counted for gasoline to return them to Abingdon. Bob and Fritz managed to hang on to Bob's dream, but just barely. The pressure of trying to make ends meet was especially hard on Fritz. Being a great deal more practical than Bob when it came to finances, she simply couldn't lose herself in the magic of the stage as could he. Despite her daily worries, she and Bob seldom quarreled about money, and for the most part she simply bit her lower lip and pinched the pennies even tighter. Bob would often return in the afternoon to their small apartment at the Barter Inn to find Fritz hunched over her account books with a half-consumed highball in her hand. At first Bob didn't recognize that Fritz, who had seldom consumed alcohol before, suffered from more and more morning "headaches." He simply marked it up to the stress of trying to make ends meet.

At the end of every summer season Bob and Fritz went back to Bob's old fourth-floor apartment on Fifty-eighth Street in New York. Bob became a member of the Players Club and did more than twenty mostly forgotten roles on Broadway during the following years. He was also beginning to make a very good living in radio, especially in live soap operas. His friend, Lula Vollmer, a successful playwright on Broadway, was writing for radio in a big way. Her mountain characters—she was from northern Georgia—peopled numerous serials such as *The Widow's Sons, Grits 'n' Gravy,* and *Moonshine and Honeysuckle.* Bob's mountain drawl was in big demand and the pay was good, but even monetary success failed to satisfy his inner hunger.

Helen Fritz, circa 1938.

Though radio gave me good friends and weekly paychecks I got to hate it, as I hate all the mechanical media which take the joy out of performance. Radio required me to give and give and give to that invisible audience which never gives anything back, and I grew in time "mike-sick." Even if I had not grown bored with radio, perhaps my Barter Theatre would have continued to force itself on me in spite of myself. Our publicity made me a character and a legend, and I began to be besieged with applicants. The theatrical world heard I was an offbeat producer who would take a chance on untried young actors. I only paid in produce, to be sure, and I worked the devil out of you, but the climate of Abingdon was reported to be wonderful. And so they began to climb the four flights of stairs to what I called my "casting couch," eight or nine hundred of them per year. They all wanted work.

Lady Luck, despite being capriciously fickle, frequently smiled on Bob Porterfield, and once she must have laughed out loud. One day Bob was hurrying down Broadway with a newspaper-wrapped Virginia ham under his arm, on his way to give it to Arthur Hopkins, the renowned and famously inaccessible producer who had arranged for Bob to present one of his plays royalty-free in Abingdon. Suddenly Bob realized he was being followed, and then he rounded a corner and came nose to nose with two of New York's finest. One of the policemen, a tall and florid-faced Irishman, pointed to his parcel and demanded, "What you got under your arm, Buddy?"

"It's a Virginia ham," said Bob. "I'm taking it to Arthur Hopkins."

They both chuckled and rolled their eyes. "Okay, Mac, let's see it."

Bob took the ham from beneath his arm right there in the middle of Broadway and unwrapped it. "Well, I'll be damned!" said the policemen who laughed broadly and apologized somewhat red-faced. Only then did it dawn on Bob—in those wild days of the great gangsters such as Dillinger, Capone, and hundreds of less-infamous ruffians—how much a wrapped Virginia ham resembled a tommy gun. He had been followed for blocks under suspicion of being on his way to a "hit" of some sort—which, as it turned out, was true, but with Bob's trademark luck and knack for being in the right place at the right time, it indeed turned out to be a "hit," but with a different definition.

He rewrapped his ham in its newspaper and hurried on to the office of Arthur Hopkins, where, forgetting the awe and intimidation that any actor in his right mind should have felt at approaching the great man, Bob burst in. The story was just too irresistible not to share. "You have just gotta hear this!" he exclaimed, then told Hopkins about the ham incident.

Hopkins shook his head, came as close to laughing as he ever had, and eyed Bob quizzically. "You come see me tomorrow afternoon," he said at last. "There's a part I might be able to use you for."

Bob was cast as Herb, a young cowboy, in Robert E. Sherwood's *The Petrified Forest*. He began rehearsals the following Monday along with Leslie Howard and Humphrey Bogart, who was appearing in his very first tough-guy role. The play opened on January 7, 1935, at the Broadhurst Theatre and ran for 197 performances through that June, for the time a remarkable feat.

Arthur Hopkins was, according to Bob, a quiet-spoken man. The secret of his success was that he cast the parts so well. His eye for talent seemed unerring. He saw in Bogart, who up until *The Petrified Forest* had played only loose-wristed, white-trousered juveniles, the force and sardonic power that launched a gangster star.

Robert Sherwood also left a lasting impression on Bob. "To work with Robert Sherwood was a rare privilege," he recalled. "One knew instinctively that he was a man and writer of great stature, but he was not dictatorial in his assurance. He came up to each one of us and said, 'If there's any line that you don't feel comfortable with as the character, change it to something you do like and show it to me. If I like it I'll keep it, and if I don't we'll work something else out.'"

The Petrified Forest went on to become a part of theatrical history, but there was one moment during the run that Bob cherished above all others. Mandy, an African American cook whom Bob and Fritz had more or less inherited with a sublet apartment, knew that Bob was in a Broadway show and she was crazy to see it. Bob managed to get her a ticket far in the back even though the play was almost sold out. She showed up early, accompanied by a little brown paper poke that contained a bottle of potent homemade gin, and immediately seated herself in the front row. As other people began coming in and claiming their seats the ushers had to move her to her assigned seat, while she protested indignantly the whole way. When finally there, however, she settled down, took off her shoes, and began nipping at her poke so that by curtain time, she was quite content and more than a little mellow.

When a friend of hers from Harlem came on stage playing the chauffeur, she announced to several rows near her, "That's Mr. Alexander. I knows him." But when Bob made his appearance her joy knew no bounds. Leaping up out of her seat, she announced to the entire theatre: "There's Bob Porterfield! I knows him! In fact, I works for him!" A roar of laughter swept the theatre and then applause. It was several minutes before the play could get back to serious business.

Bob stayed with *The Petrified Forest* through its close in June, and then he directed a low-budget production of the play that went around in the Subway Circuit, which included the suburbs and outskirts of New York City. After that, he and Fritz returned to Abingdon for Barter's summer season. The year 1935 would finally begin to see an upswing in the economy, and cash receipts made up 20 percent of the box office that year.

It was the same year, however, in which yet another crisis threatened to destroy the fledgling theatre. An investor, thinking that the Martha Washington buildings might make a fine luxury hotel, made a deal to rent the buildings for cash, thus making the theatre company once again homeless. Just when all hope seemed lost for the theatre's future, the businesspeople of Abingdon came through and arranged for Bob and his operation to move to the abandoned campus of Abingdon's other school, the Stonewall Jackson Institute, owned by the Presbyterian synod. There were no strings attached, and since the buildings would still belong to the Presbyterians, Barter didn't even have to pay taxes. Once again, Bob's dream had been saved by his personality, blind luck, and—who could deny it now?—Saint Rita.

In the hills of Southwest Virginia, light and funny fare such as Lula Vollmer's warm and sweet *The Hill Between* was what the audiences wanted and what the actors gave them, but when Bob returned to New York that fall, light and funny was out; intense and angry was in. During that winter of discontent, 1935–36, Bob became a founding member of the Actors Repertory Company. This band of generally hungry and unemployed young actors, including a young and unknown Will Geer, was convinced that a permanent repertory company based on the European model with no individual stars would set the new standard for Broadway. The company ended up lasting for only two years, but it was enough to firmly convince Bob that the concept was basically sound—that a group working together closely could produce better theatre in the long run than could productions based around one well-known and expensive star performer.

The ARC's first production was a southern play, but unlike *The Hill Between*, *Let Freedom Ring* was a bitter indictment of the closing of cotton mills and was anything but warm and funny. It would never have lasted in Abingdon, but in New York City was a hit despite mixed reviews. *Hymn to the Rising Sun*, about the brutality of a mixed black and white North Carolina chain gang, came next, but it closed quickly for lack of support. The company's next play, *Bury the Dead*, was a hit as it aroused savage controversy.

First Lady Eleanor Roosevelt was a strong supporter of the Actors Repertory Company both in her patronage and in her widely read newspaper column. She went to see *Bury the Dead* and, much to the chagrin of the theatre's management, insisted on paying for her own ticket. Since Bob knew Mrs. Roosevelt from the time she had visited Virginia's Whitetop Mountain Folk Festival in 1933, the rest of the cast asked him to go out into the audience and invite her backstage to see them after the show.

"Bob, this is a play everybody in the country ought to see," she proclaimed. "Why don't you do it at your theatre in Abingdon?"

Bury the Dead was angry, cruel, and full of the playwright's hatred of war.

"Mrs. Roosevelt," Bob replied, "I don't think they can take it down there."

"They can take it, all right," she stated bluntly. "They've got to take it. It's against war."

> I spent a lot of time thinking over her advice. It is hard to be a daring and experimental producer when your box office line is quite literally your breadline. We had no cash in reserve with which to ignore the public tastes. But I, too, had been deeply

> impressed with *Bury the Dead* and the message it carried. All
> right, I decided, we'll do the play, and we'll do it right, with all the
> "hell"s and "God"s and "damn"s left in. If people object to it, I
> can always blame it on Mrs. Roosevelt.

Bob held his breath, but *Bury the Dead* kept Barter audiences spell-
bound. Even with its grim impact and message, it turned out to be an
unqualified success. Newspapers as well as patrons labeled it Barter's
best production to date. Thanks to Mrs. Roosevelt's faith in Southwest Virginia theatregoers, Bob found the courage to put on other
plays that he liked and thought important, no matter what the subject
might be. In the process, he said, he thought he educated Barter patrons to become one of the best audiences in the United States.

He even began—judiciously—to leave in the "hell"s and "damn"s,
but he always kept the advice of his grandfather in mind when it
came to swearing. His grandfather was an avid bear hunter and often
spent weeks traipsing the wild mountains with Grayson County's
famed bear hunter, Wilburn Waters.

> I often have occasion to remember what my grandfather told me
> when I was a little boy. My grandfather was, I suppose, really
> one of the vanishing Virginians. I doubt whether he ever did a
> lick of work in his life, but his shoulders were wide, his face was
> gay, and he rode a horse as though he were sitting in a rocking
> chair, with perfect ease. To my grandfather, cursing was part of
> his generation. The profanity that flowed from his lips with such
> eloquence, such poise, could hardly be duplicated today with-
> out sounding vulgar. But when I tried to imitate him I got into trou-
> ble. "Robert," he told me, "if you can't curse convincingly, just
> don't curse."

Bob lost a few customers, of course, but he felt that he gained more
than he lost, and that the ones he gained were better-educated and
more open to innovation than the ones who left. A local fire-and-
brimstone revivalist named Dan Graham kept on berating the actors and "that wicked cesspool of iniquity" that was Barter, but Bob
soon noticed that every time the good reverend came to town with
his tent and tirades, theatre attendance went up. Bob said that
he liked to think his spirit of artistic adventure was wearing off on

Abingdon. One of his brothers, Graham, who was at that time in the fertilizer business, told Bob that the two of them had a lot in common. "We're both spreading improvement."

In 1937, Bob felt confident enough about his theatre to raise admission to forty cents, and at the end of the season annual profit had leaped from 1933's $4.35 to a whopping $60. That year, seventy actors put on fourteen plays and racked up more than six thousand miles on Barter's rickety fleet of fourteen trucks and buses. Even with such affluence, the entire Barter company continued to be paid in whatever barter brought in. Only local people hired to cook, clean, and do similar jobs were paid in cash. An astute local preacher—not the Reverend Graham—told Bob that if church people worked as hard as Bob's actors, the devil would have "one hell of a time of it."

Although Fritz began to struggle more and more, Bob was having the time of his life. "I was happier than I had ever been," he said, "auditioning, acting, directing, guiding the activities of three stock companies at once and continually passing the hat to keep my theatre alive." A few times he attempted to talk to Fritz about her worsening state of mind, but she steadfastly denied she was drinking any more than usual.

Bob, probably like every person who has ever worked in New York theatre, began to think that he wanted to produce a Broadway show. In the fall of 1937 he got his chance. Lula Vollmer, whose *The Hill Between* Bob had premiered at Barter, managed to talk a Broadway angel into giving her ten thousand dollars to stage the production in New York, and she then convinced Bob to be the producer. It opened in March 1938 at the Little Theatre on West Forty-fourth Street. While the play wasn't a complete flop, it received tepid reviews at best and only ran for three weeks. The production broke even, but just barely. The experience, primarily with the off-stage unions, cured Bob forever of wanting to produce on Broadway.

Producing in New York was cold and brutal, strangled by cut-throat competition, the ruthless pressure of time, and the theatrical unions. To begin with, about a quarter of our budget was earmarked for scenery, and the rest of the money was going down the drain for people I didn't want. You have to hire two public relations people whether you need two public relations people or not, you have to hire people from the stagehands union and people from the music union, and, before you know it, you are running out of money. The last person to be remembered is the actor, and I ended up hiring a two-hundred-dollar actor instead of the one-thousand-dollar actor I had wanted.

It is the front-of-the-house unions, the nonperforming ones, who take so much and give so little, that I resent the most. They tried to get us down in Abingdon, too, but I was a little more successful there in giving the slip to their unreasonable demands. Once Petrillo, czar of the music publishing and recording world, tried to catch me by asking what kind of music we used for our productions at Barter Theatre. "Oh, we just hum," I said.

While I was producing *The Hill Between* I would want to go out in the lobby and speak to people as they came in, or tell them goodnight as they left, the way I did back home, and my publicity man would say, "No, you can't do that. This is New York; people don't do that sort of thing here." I wanted to go into the box office and count up the house, and my union box office man would say, "No, you can't do that. This is New York; we don't work that way here." I finally got fed up with the whole thing and said, "To hell with this—I'm not having any fun!" If you can't have fun with the theatre in New York, I decided, I'm going back to Abingdon where I can pull the curtain if I want to and act if I want to and count the house if I want to and, by damn, even move the scenery if I want to. That was the last Broadway saw of me as a producer.

Bob continued to produce at his own theatre, however, especially new plays by frequently unknown playwrights. Barter, from its very first year, always tried to stage two or three new plays a summer, most of them world premieres. One of the reasons for this, Bob admitted, was that he could produce the plays of new or unknown playwrights without royalty other than a Virginia ham, but the real reason was that he always believed that a repertory theatre has just as much responsibility for discovering and encouraging new playwrights as it has for discovering and encouraging new actors. Bob quoted Eugene O'Neill, who once said that if one wishes to write for the theatre, he should pick up his hammer and join one. In 1938

Bob decided to host a resident playwright for the summer, so he asked his friend Audrey Wood, a well-known agent who represented playwrights, if she knew of any unknown writer she would recommend. She suggested two, and Bob chose Arnold Sundgaard. He stayed with Barter off and on for several years, and Bob produced four of his plays. He went on to moderate success, but one of his plays—which he wrote during a winter that he and his wife spent in a tiny cabin high atop Whitetop Mountain and which was called *Virginia Overture*—became the first American play to be translated into German and broadcast after World War II over the powerful Radio Frankfurt to tell occupied Germany what American freedom was like.

Sundgaard's commercial success was relatively unremarkable, but he won several Guggenheim awards and fellowships. Bob suspected that the fellowships might have been the reason Sundgaard's craft never matured into what he believed it could have been. "I am a great believer in actors and writers—all people in the creative arts, in fact—suffering for their art," said Bob. "I sometimes wonder if more genius has been killed than created by subsidy. I doubt if Arnold Sundgaard has written anything since quite so good as what he wrote when he was living on Whitetop, reading Shakespeare aloud by the fire, and walking a twenty-two-mile roundtrip to mail a manuscript."

The other young playwright recommended by Audrey Wood, the one Bob did not select, apparently had to suffer a bit more, because nearly every play he wrote went on to both critical and commercial success. His name was Tennessee Williams.

As the world spiraled out of control into what would soon become World War II, Bob and Barter Theatre staged its most ambitious production ever and arguably still its most successful. It was about another war, a conflict even more brutal than World War II in which even more Americans, nearly a million, died—two-thirds of them slowly and painfully from infection and disease. The play was *Lee of Virginia*, and it was about the War Between the States.

Even combining Barter's three touring companies for a total of eighty actors and technicians, some performers had to play multiple roles. One unknown young man in his first year of professional acting played abolitionist John Brown in the first act, but played Confederate General Stonewall Jackson in the third. A newspaper reviewer captured the moment: "One of the best scenes and the most dramatic," the reviewer wrote, "was John Brown's interview with General Lee at Harper's Ferry." The actor who played John Brown as well as General Jackson was singled out for praise. Said the reviewer, "Gregory Peck was thrilling."

For the gala opening night, Bob invited the only two Confederate veterans still alive in the area, General Julius Howe, aged ninety-three, and Private John Wilson, aged ninety-six, to attend. Both men had actually served under General Robert E. Lee. This knowledge did little to lessen the nervousness of Dick Woodruff, the young actor who was playing Lee.

Bob had put out the word for his opening-night patrons to come dressed in costumes that would have been worn during the War Between the States, and they enthusiastically took him up on his request. People arrived wearing crinolines and hoop skirts of the antebellum South; they arrived in limousines, farm trucks, wagons, and even a pony cart, and they marched into the theatre to the rousing sounds of a brass band playing "Dixie." Bob escorted his two old veterans to the center of the front row so he could bring them onstage after the show and introduce them.

Bob later said that it was on that night that he fully realized that theatre is above all a personal thing and that it provides a satisfaction and an audience involvement that no form of canned entertainment will ever be able to replace. Only a live production such as *Lee of Virginia* has the power to bring the flesh and blood of history right into the hearts of the audience.

At the final curtain call with all the actors onstage, Bob brought up the two old veterans and was just preparing to introduce them to the actors and the audience when Private John Wilson, almost a century old, broke away from Bob and shuffled across the stage toward General Lee. Drawing himself up to ramrod-straight attention, the old warrior saluted as smartly as any young soldier ever did and said, "Sir, I was on my way to Appomattox to help you when you surrendered. Why didn't you wait?"

But the story has a sequel. Not long after *Lee of Virginia* closed,

America was plunged into World War II, and the men and women who had performed at Barter were soon scattered across the globe. Arthur Frantz, who had been in the Barter company during 1939, was aboard an Army Air Corps C-117 transport flying the hump into China during the closing days of the war. Frantz knew no one on board the airplane, but the route was extremely dangerous and to relieve the tension he related the story he had heard to some of the other passengers and crew.

"It's a nice story," scoffed the airplane's radioman when Frantz was finished, "but I don't believe it."

That was when the pilot turned away from his instrument panel. "You can believe it or not," said Captain Dick Woodruff, "but it is true. I was the actor playing General Lee."

10

Where Does This Boy Belong?

Though Bob and his company tried to lose themselves in hard work, the darkening shadows of the war in Europe in 1940 draped like a cold, wet blanket over all of them. The young male actors were more serious, trying to squeeze every last benefit out of every minute of the summer's work. The actresses were equally apprehensive and seemed to write far more letters home than before. A few of Barter's former company members were already in uniform, everyone knew, and the very air itself seemed to crackle with a different spirit. It was far from unusual now for the actors to spot uniforms in their audiences. More patrons were able to buy their admissions with cash, thanks to a booming war economy, but gasoline, diesel fuel, and tires were in short supply. Touring was curtailed drastically.

Bob continued the annual Barter Theatre Award Luncheons in New York City that he had started in 1939, in which he presented a Virginia ham to the actor or actress voted to have made the most memorable contribution to theatre during the previous year. Thanks to Bob's personality and contacts, the luncheon always included some of Broadway's most famous people as well as such well-known nonactors as Eleanor Roosevelt, who presented the first award. The award also included a handmade platter "to eat the ham off of" and the deed to an acre of near-vertical Virginia mountain land not far from Twin Oaks. In addition to the ham, the platter, and the rocky mountainside, the person honored was entitled to pick two unknown actors—one male, one female—to go to Barter for the summer. Several of these young people went on to become famous: Larry Gates, Gregory Peck, Mitchell Ryan, and others.

By then Bob had become a luncheon speaker of some note with an agent who booked him all over the country. On one of his visits to California, he looked up Geoffrey Lind, a former Barter actor who was a rising star in Hollywood using the name of Jeffrey Lynn. He told Bob that Warner Brothers was starting to make a film about the life of Sergeant Alvin York, the pacifist Tennessee hero of the Great War, later to be known as World War I. The producer, Jesse Lasky, asked Bob if he would read for the part of Zeb Andrews, and before he realized what was happening Bob had signed a contract. Directed by Howard Hawks, the film starred Gary Cooper, the only actor whom Alvin York would allow to portray him.

At the premiere of *Sergeant York* in Washington, D.C., Bob found himself seated beside the real Sergeant York and his wife, Miss Gracie, along with their son, Woodrow Wilson York. The press crowded around York, snapping pictures and trying unsuccessfully to get him to comment on the movie or his reaction to seeing his life on film. When the premiere was over, the Yorks and Bob boarded the same Southern Railroad train that evening—Bob for Abingdon, and the Yorks for their home in Pall Mall, Tennessee. The next morning the three of them met in the dining car over breakfast. They began talking about the movie, and Mrs. York chided her husband gently. "Alvin, they had scenes in that movie of your drinking," she said. "I never knew you to touch a drop."

"Well, Gracie," he replied, "I had too much respect for you to ever let you see me in that condition." Then he turned to Bob. "You know that scene in the movie when the lightning hit me and knocked me off the mule? That actually happened to me. And when I picked myself up and realized I was still alive, I was so thankful I took an oath I would never drink again or curse again or fight again. The only one of them pledges I ever broke was when they came and convinced me I should fight, I fit."

Bob looked Alvin York in the eye. "I know you wouldn't tell the press what you thought of the movie," he said, "but I wish you'd tell me."

York looked thoughtful. "Mark Twain went with some friends to see the Atlantic Ocean for the first time," he said. "Someone kept asking him, 'Well, what do you think?' He kept looking at it, staring out over the breaking waves, and finally he said, 'It appears to be a success.'"

Bob continued his tour of speaking engagements after the 1941 summer season, but he was in New York on December 7, 1941. He said that he could remember being in a theatre that evening, but even though the play was billed as a hilarious comedy no one was laughing very much. They had just learned that Japan had bombed Pearl Harbor and that the United States had been finally drawn into World War II.

A few weeks later Bob was invited to join the Special Services, but he refused. Even though entertaining was his business, he wanted to be a fighting soldier in the defense of his country instead of just one of a band of, he said, "unspontaneous merry makers who forced good humor down the throats of privates." He wanted to serve as an officer in the U.S. Navy and tried to get a commission but with no success, even though Charles J. Harkrader, a prominent business-man, wrote a letter of recommendation to the navy. "You couldn't find a finer type of man, everything considered, than Robert Porter-field," he wrote. "We are apt to think of actors as persons in a dif-ferent category from most of the rest of us, but Bob Porterfield is a man's man and is exceptionally well qualified in my judgment to be Navy officer material."

Whatever its reasons, the navy still wasn't interested, so Bob decided to await his draft call and just take his chances. In the meantime he went about his business of lecturing, radio work, and planning the upcoming season in Abingdon—in case there still was to be one.

The 1942 season was Barter's tenth and one of its toughest. Bob and Fritz arrived in Abingdon to find the Stonewall Jackson prop-erty, which they had been allowed to use rent-free, no longer va-cant. It had been turned into a U.S. Army regional induction center where draftees and volunteers were brought from all over Appa-lachia for their examinations, shots, and preliminary indoctrina-tions. The theatre in the old town hall was still available, however, and the owner of a rambling old house named Greenway Haven just outside of Abingdon told Bob and Fritz they could use it to board the actors. They decided to go ahead and try to play the season, although with severe gasoline rationing any plans to tour shows on the road, even close by, were abandoned.

Many of the actors of prior years had enlisted or been drafted, but according to Bob, the crop of actresses in 1942 was exceptional. It included Jocelyn Brando, Marlon Brando's sister, and a beautiful teenager named Patricia Neal, whom the drama critic of the Knoxville newspaper had recommended. To utilize all the female talent, Bob presented a number of plays calling for strong female casts, including *Letters to Lucerne* and the premiere of Edie Sommers's first play, *No Boys Allowed*. Bob realized that his public during the summer of 1942 wanted to temporarily forget the war and laugh, so he staged comedies such as *The Man Who Came to Dinner*, *There's Always Juliet*, and *French without Tears*.

Every year on the closing night of the season after the final curtain, it had been a tradition for the entire company to gather on stage and drink a "loving cup" together. The loving cup wasn't all that grand by most standards, being a quart Mason jar of pure corn liquor, but Bob thought it very much in keeping with the mountains. The first quart had been bartered for a ticket in 1939, and as the level went down in the jar, one or another of Bob's many mountaineer acquaintances would drop by and top it off for him.

On that August night late in the summer of 1942, with a cool breeze wafting the scent of an early autumn through the opened backstage doors, the company sat on the stage and somberly passed around the jar, with each person taking a sip of moonshine straight from the container. There was a little effort at levity, but more tears than laughter. Everyone seemed to be trying to avoid looking at everyone else, because they knew—as did Bob—that it was the last time some of them would ever be on a stage. In the years 1943, 1944, and 1945, there would be no Barter Theatre at all. In March 1943, Bob received greetings in a letter from his government. His next role, a command performance, was to be as Private Robert H. Porterfield, U.S. Army.

He was in California when his draft letter showed up at the apartment in New York City. Fritz called him with the news. Over the crackling long-distance telephone wires, Bob could hear both the fear and the weakness in her voice. He realized they were slipping further and further apart, but now, even if he had known what he could do to try to salvage their life together, the war had taken the future out of his hands.

On the day he learned that he had been drafted, always the trouper, Bob went ahead and presented his scheduled talk to a woman's club in Santa Barbara.

> I remember the engagement vividly, for on the night before I was supposed to speak on "Hams for Playwrights," the oil storage depots along the shoreline had been mysteriously shelled. Everyone thought the Japanese had done it. Under the circumstance, I hardly expected anyone to turn out to hear me, but to my surprise the auditorium was packed. The good ladies, eager to prove they weren't afraid, anxious to see and be seen by anyone else who dared to appear, turned out in unrivaled numbers; some even came in wheelchairs. There was an electric tension in the air; we all tried not to listen for a return of the explosions. I went ahead speaking about Barter Theatre and the dreams I had for it when we should once again be able to turn our minds and hearts back to the niceties of life.

Bob spoke to the assembled ladies about his vision for a theatre decentralized away from Broadway, of how he dreamed that Barter Theatre in Virginia could encourage the birth of similar theatres in each of the other forty-seven states. When he was finished, one of the women in the audience, Mrs. Amory Hare Hutchinson, went up to him and said, "The thing you're talking about is the very reason Congress gave a federal charter to the American National Theatre and Academy eight years ago. It's just been sitting there ever since. Why don't you do something about it?" For the moment, Bob forgot her words, but he would remember them later.

Because he was already in California, Bob received permission to report for induction at Fort MacArthur in San Pedro, a gritty little port town south of Los Angeles, instead of traveling back to Virginia's Fort Lee. He went through the barrage of aptitude tests and inoculations as well as the venereal disease films and lectures that the military felt so important for men about to storm beaches and charge German machine guns. After hours of standing in line, he finally reached the station where he was to be interviewed so that the army could figure out which job might best fit him. Bob went in expecting to discuss the slots available with an officer but found himself facing a newly minted private just like himself.

"Sit down, Porterfield," the private ordered. Bob sat. The private asked what hobbies Bob had.

"Watercress, horses, and people," Bob replied. This answer seemed to throw the private off-step for a second, but with a much-chewed pencil he dutifully scribbled Bob's answer down onto a form. He asked a few more questions, recorded the answers, and then asked Bob what, just exactly, did Bob think he could offer the armed services. Bob replied that he thought his background more or less qualified him for the liaison field.

"What?"

"Liaison," Bob repeated.

"How do you spell it?"

"L-i-a-i-s-o-n."

The private reached into his desk, extracted a dog-eared paperback Webster's dictionary, and thumbed through it. A few seconds later he looked up at Bob with an expression as if he wanted to kill him.

"Are you trying to pull my leg?" the private snorted. Bob said no, puzzled by the private's anger.

The private slammed the dictionary down on the desk. "In here, it says 'liaison—an illicit relation between a man and a woman'!"

The next day Bob was shipped out to a cavalry unit at Fort Riley, Kansas.

Bob had comfortably worn a lieutenant's uniform in the film *Army Chaplain* (in an uncredited part), but the uniform of a private at Fort Riley wore far less easily. For one thing, officers rode while Bob and the other privates marched and trained on foot. His basic training turned out to be more about manure forks and shovels than about rifles and hand grenades. Grabbing a few seconds between equine KP duties, he wrote to James Hilton, the author of *Goodbye, Mr. Chips* and *Lost Horizon*, whom he had met a year or so earlier. Bob complained with as much humor as he could muster about the odor of the army as he was getting to know it. Hilton straight away mailed him a small bottle of Chanel No. 5, but according to Bob, it only encouraged the horses.

At Fort Riley Bob had plenty of opportunity to see the type of entertainment the government was offering its armed forces. The playwright Robert Sherwood, who was in Washington, D.C., serving as an advisor to President Roosevelt, wrote Bob and asked him to do a little unofficial survey to find out what the men wanted in the way of Special Services activities.

Bob wrote back:

> Twenty-five percent of the men, the noisiest and most vocal, belong to what I call the "gutter" group. Their idea of entertainment is a good guffaw. Twenty percent of the others, for whom nothing is done at this time, have discrimination and taste and would enjoy good music, books, and theatre. I think the rest can either be elevated to the level of the men of good taste or dropped to the gutter group, all according to what is offered them.

The army, Bob wrote Sherwood, seemed to be catering exclusively to the first group. All the men had in the way of entertainment at Fort Riley was, Bob reported, "titillating girlie shows with lots of legs, then sex lectures the next morning." He wrote that the physical recreation facilities were splendid, but the opportunities for cultural recreation were almost nonexistent. The Special Services, he concluded, in offering crude and lewd shows thought it was giving all the men what they wanted, but Bob begged for some recognition of people like himself who wanted a recreation not found in guffaws. And wouldn't it be a splendid opportunity for men of the theatre, he asked, with this vast captive audience, to stimulate appreciation for the finer arts?

Bob never knew for sure if his little survey actually set any wheels in motion, but he did notice that not long thereafter, Special Services sent Katherine Cornell, arguably Broadway's top actress of the time, on a tour of army bases in *The Barrets of Wimpole Street*, and the success of that effort led to Maurice Evans's all-G.I. *Hamlet*. Full-length plays began to take a place beside the leg shows, and many great artists of the theatre were enlisted to tour for service personnel in America and abroad. The burlesque entertainment never lost its appeal for the bulk of American soldiers, marines, and sailors, of course, but at least there was finally a little choice.

Meanwhile, in the stables of Fort Riley, Bob had grown pretty tired of shoveling horse manure, so he turned to letter writing for diversion. One of the people he wrote to was Frank McCarthy, whom he had known in their Broadway days and who was now a member of General George Marshall's advisory staff in Washington, D.C. He recited the story of his attempt to break into the l-i-a-i-s-o-n business because he felt McCarthy would find it amusing. He had a hunch that army privates would be frowned upon for writing letters to colonels, so he marked it "private." Not until after V-J Day did Bob finally hear what had transpired.

On the day that McCarthy received Bob's letter, he was on his way to a staff meeting with General Marshall, and he took the letter along to read while he was waiting. He opened it and let out a whoop of laughter. Bernard Baruch, one of Roosevelt's top economic advisors, passing by on his way to an appointment with the president, wanted to know what was so funny. Frank could not resist handing him the letter. Baruch read it, folded it, and announced, "Franklin has got to see this." He went in a few minutes later, and McCarthy reported he had never heard such a shout of laughter as came out of the president's office. Roosevelt personally returned the letter to McCarthy a short time later and asked, "Frank, where does this boy belong?"

All Bob knew of any of this at the time was that one afternoon a few days before his unit was due to be shipped out, while he was practicing target shooting on the rifle range, a voice came over the loudspeaker. "Private Robert Porterfield . . . Private Robert Porterfield will report to headquarters." Bob marched to headquarters apprehensively. He knew he had been doing pretty badly at target shooting, and he fully expected to be chewed out and assigned more manure to shovel. Instead of a reprimand he was told to pack his gear; he was being shipped out the next day. He was put on a train heading west, and his orders were to report to such-and-such an address in Culver City, California. He duly reported to the address given, a low green Quonset hut, and presented himself to the sergeant on duty. The noncom stared at Bob's orders in amazement and then asked, "How did you get here?"

"On the train."

"I mean, who sent you? Where do you come from? Who do you know? Three thousand men have been waiting and politicking to get into this unit for weeks, and you just walk in on orders."

Only then did Bob discover that he had been assigned to the army's First Motion Picture Unit. He was to join David Wayne, William Holden, Ronald Reagan, Norman Krasner, Arthur Kennedy, John Beale, George Oppenheimer, and a score of others in the prize assignment of making training and indoctrination films for the Army Air Force.

Less than a week later, Bob's old unit at Fort Riley was shipped out to North Africa, like so many young Americans hurled green into a war they were not yet ready to fight. Less than a dozen members of his unit ever returned.

11

An Extra Row of Beans

Culver City was in the 1940s one of Hollywood's suburbs with palm trees, warm breezes, and clear blue skies seldom bothered by clouds. Though only a private in rank, Bob began to enjoy an active social life. He and his colleagues in the First Motion Picture Unit were allowed to live off-base, and Bob discovered that his friend James Hilton owned a lovely apartment building close to the studios. He and five other soldiers went together and rented a large flat that was vacant. Alice Hilton, who was at the time divorced from James Hilton, seemed to know everybody, and she frequently organized informal get-togethers of former Barter actors such as Gregory Peck and Bill Prince, who were by then rising Hollywood stars. She and Bob quickly became good friends, and he frequently filled the role of co-host when she entertained.

The fact that Bob, a private, was frequently called upon to play the role of an officer in the films he was making sometimes led to interesting situations. The rule was that when going to or from the set dressed in the uniform of an officer, the enlisted men were supposed to carry their hats or caps in their hands, thereby marking them as faux brass, but this strategy didn't always work. One of the films Bob made required him to dress as an army major. During filming, a real major, Myron Balch, who was a scriptwriter, was in the habit of dropping by the set and chatting with Bob whenever he wasn't busy. One day he told Bob he would like him to meet his wife and family and issued a dinner invitation.

That evening Bob showed up at the major's home, properly dressed in his private's uniform. When Balch came to the door he took one look at Bob and needed all his powers of decorum not to fall over backward. Only then did both realize that the real major had never seen Bob off the set and had assumed the two were equal in rank. All they could do was laugh. Despite military regulations forbidding fraternization between officers and enlisted men, their friendship ripened; the Culver City people were, after all, not exactly the most regimental types.

Balch invited Bob to take part in his choice of one or the other of two special projects he currently had in the works. One was to go to India to make a training movie; the other was traveling to Alaska to film *How to Land and Live in Glacial Regions*, a survival training package for Army Air Corps personnel. Bob had often read books about the Klondike territory and had once performed in an Actors Repertory Company production of *200 Were Chosen*, a play set in the Far North. With Saint Rita still in his pocket, he chose the assignment to Alaska.

The group of actors and technicians assigned to the other mission, the one to India, never reached its destination. An enemy fighter shot down their airplane en route. No one survived.

Bob had high hopes that the film his crew was assigned to make would prove vitally important in training pilots and crews. The United States, having realized Alaska's strategic importance in the event of a Japanese invasion through the Aleutian Islands, which they actually attempted at Dutch Harbor, was sinking millions of dollars into defense preparation and survival bases, and the pilots desperately needed the information Bob and his team were preparing to document. The mission quickly became, in the words of GIs, FUBAR—fouled up beyond all recognition. Washington had sent the film crew out at precisely the wrong time of year, in midwinter when at best there were three hours a day even remotely bright enough for filming . . . and that was on days when blinding blizzards didn't shut down operations altogether.

They hunkered down in one corner of a small aircraft hangar and waited for several months until a quarter-million dollars worth of equipment was flown to Brady Glacier and dropped by brilliantly colored cargo parachutes so the crew could easily find it. The men traveled by boat to the glacier a day or two later as soon

Bob discusses how to shoot a scene in an Army Air Corps training film on a soundstage at Culver City, California.

as the seas were calm enough. They climbed up onto the great creaking river of ice, only to discover that a blizzard and drifting snow had covered everything so completely that they were never able to find so much as a trace of the equipment. Bob often remarked that, centuries hence, a piece of that glacier will finally break off and some future archaeologists are going to have a tough time trying to figure out why all that antique moviemaking gear came to be embedded in an iceberg.

Without equipment, the mission had to be scrubbed, but it had given Bob and his fellow crew members the chance to see a wild Alaska that few have experienced. He reveled in the magnificent scale, the seemingly endless virgin forests, the rock and ice and the roiling black Bering Sea. They returned to Culver City and made the survival film inside a Hollywood ice house as, according to Bob, it should have been done to begin with.

In February 1944, not long after he completed the arctic survival film, Bob received a letter from home advising him that his father was very ill and not expected to live. Bob's commanding officer gave him permission to go home to see his father, but something, perhaps his bit of Cherokee heritage, told him that the time had not yet come. Bob told this to his commanding officer and asked if he might be authorized to take his leave when he sensed it was time. The officer looked at him strangely but gave the permission he requested. A few weeks later Bob woke up knowing that the time had come. He hitchhiked a ride on an army airplane heading east and was, it turned out, the only one of W. B. Porterfield's sons who was with him when he died.

Bob knew that he had gone against his father's wishes when he entered the theatre. It was not out of any lack of love or respect for his father, but rather out of the insistent demand of his whole being. He had never ceased to hope that he might win the elder Porterfield over to his enterprise. W. B. Porterfield had never been openly hostile to Bob and his people, but the only reason he turned his surplus produce over to help feed them was because the only alternative was to watch it rot. He had never ceased to disclaim any financial interest in his son's frivolous dreams, but he began going to every Barter production and he seemed to more or less enjoy them. He continued to wonder, however, when or if his son was ever going to find something to do to make a living.

In 1936, W. B. Porterfield had come to the theatre to see *Candida*, and the play seemed to stir some forgotten memories from his youth. He never told Bob what it might have been, but he did admit that *Candida* was the best thing he had ever seen on stage. The ice of his reserve seemed to melt away after that, and W.B. began to see actors as people. Just before he passed away he told Bob, "Robert, the people in the theatre are just as nice as anybody else, only more so."

"It was an impressive tribute to the quality of the ladies and gentlemen I had brought to our Bible Belt," Bob reminisced, "and it came from the person I most wanted to hear it from."

That turned out to be the only bright spot in an otherwise sorrowful visit.

In addition to losing his father, Bob discovered that his theatre just a month earlier had also been struck a powerful blow that for all practical purposes had destroyed it. Tornados are possible but

Barter Theatre workshop destroyed by 1944 tornado. All the props, sets, and lights were also destroyed.

very rare in the Virginia highlands. Usually, the rolling hills break up their destructive force before they have a chance to travel far, but in a purely freak act of nature one had cut a narrow swath across Abingdon and had struck the Stonewall Jackson property head-on. No one was in the buildings, and not one single person in Abingdon received so much as a scratch, but the gymnasium full of Bob's scenery, lighting equipment, and stage properties was demolished. People picked up fragments of scenery and spotlights miles away. The beautiful white-columned porches of the dormitories had been ripped away, and one entire brick wall of a building had collapsed. The lawns and golf course were a sea of mud, and centuries-old trees had been ripped out by their roots and toppled. Bob's mother, Miss Daisy, even in her concern for her dying husband, had found the time and strength to gather up what little of her son's things had survived and stored them in a small garage, but it was a pitiful sight compared to the well-stocked scene dock Bob had so carefully secured two seasons earlier.

He traveled back to Culver City sick at heart. Bob had never stopped hoping that once the maelstrom of war had passed he could gather up some of the old Barter people, bring in fresh talent, and carry on as before. Capricious Nature seemed to have wrenched that decision out of his hands.

Barter dormitory, with its end blown off by the tornado.

For awhile Bob worked on establishment of a Veterans Theatre that might function like the old Chautauqua circuit, taking legitimate theatre to towns and hamlets all over the country, but faced with raging apathy he finally abandoned the idea. The army establishment had never approved of his ideas about a theatre to employ veterans, and when somebody complained that Bob was using his franking privileges to promote the idea of a Veterans Theatre, he was forced to reimburse the government six hundred dollars for the postage he had used.

One of the people he had been corresponding with about his idea was Eleanor Roosevelt, so when he was granted a furlough to visit his mother in Virginia, he made a side trip by the White House to meet with Mrs. Roosevelt. When his officers back in Culver City found out he had visited the White House without securing official army permission, he was unceremoniously reassigned to Shepherd Field, known then as the army's Siberia, in Wichita Falls, Texas. For five of the most boring weeks of his life Bob cooled his heels in arid northern Texas with the mesquite and armadillos. The only relief was when he went down to Fort Worth with some civilian friends to see the opera *Carmen*. It was late when he returned to base, and a sentry demanded to know where he had been.

"I've been to see *Carmen*," Bob told him.

The sentry's interest immediately perked up. He winked and waved Bob through the gate, but ever the good soldier, the sentry felt obligated to advise Bob that he should go by the medical corpsmen's office in a day or two to be checked for syphilis.

Bob's exile came to an end when his friend Rex Smith, in charge of public relations for the Army Signal Corps, arranged for him to be transferred to the First Radio Unit in New York City with offices just a short hike from Broadway. Bob had not been in New York City for more than two and a half years, and Fritz had moved back to Pennsylvania to live with her parents until the war was over.

New York City had hardly gone into hibernation. Instead of being suspended in time as Bob might have suspected it would be, the city was bustling with activity, lights, and prosperity. Every theatre was crowded, and every available ticket was being sold. Apparently businesspeople, members of the military, and military dependents were anxious for the diversion that plays provided.

Even though the war seemed to be winding down, Bob was assigned to undergo an extensive and very demanding training course in radio techniques that would enable his unit to go into combat areas and record the action. Midway through the course his training was interrupted, and he was flown to Akron, Ohio, and put on a special task force to record one of America's first jets taking off and landing. Bob had to actually lie on the ground directly under the jet's trajectory as it took off. He was scared to death most of the time, but he did make his recordings and returned safely to New York.

When he arrived back in New York he found out that a pattern set twice before in his military career had continued; while he was in Ohio, his radio unit had been unexpectedly shipped out to the Pacific war zone. A Japanese fighter shot down their plane, and when it crashed into the South Pacific, all aboard perished.

By Christmas 1944 the war seemed to be creeping toward its end, although many months of hard fighting and thousands of casualties still lay ahead. For Germany the end would come in April 1945 (V-E or Victory in Europe Day), and for Japan in August

Bob and his brothers all served in the military. (L-r) Frank, L.B., Bill, Bob, and Graham.

(V-J Day). The costliest war in history to date would be over.

In the meantime, Bob was assigned to another unit, this one in Greenwich, Connecticut. Together with Bob Breen, he briefly became interested once again in forming a national theatre, but the idea pretty much arrived stillborn for lack of funding. He was in Connecticut when word came that President Roosevelt had died, but Bob was back in New York making a recording in the NBC studios on V-J Day. He happened to be the only man in uniform in the entire building when word of the war's end arrived over the wires. Everyone began running up to Bob, hugging and kissing him, and he protested in vain, "But it wasn't me who won the war!"

Afterward, he went to his commanding officer and told him, "I could hardly wait to get into this war because I thought they couldn't win it without me. Now it looks like they've won it in spite of me. Why don't you let me go home?" The officer grinned, and a few days later Bob received his discharge papers.

The army's policy was to return discharged military members to where they had been signed up, so Bob caught a hop to Los Angeles aboard a military transport. His discharge was processed there by a soldier who would soon become a movie icon: Robert Mitchum.

Bob Porterfield was once again a civilian, now loose in the movie capital of the world. Gregory Peck was almost ready to begin making a film of Marjorie Rawlings's popular novel *The Yearling*, and Bob was hired to play an uncredited part, the second mate. According to Bob, "My part was small, and a good part of it was left on the cutting-room floor, but it gave me eight weeks that amounted to a vacation under the hanging moss of Arrowhead, California, moss transplanted from the Everglades of Florida. I began to bask in Hollywood's rarefied atmosphere."

Used to surviving on a private's pittance, Bob was making money and relishing his new affluence. He also enjoyed seeing his old friends. But Hollywood has a way of sucking in those fortunate or unfortunate enough to be caught up in its whirling kaleidoscope. As talent scouts and agents began courting Bob and talking about his next pictures, his dreams of a small live theatre back in Virginia began to fade. "I stood poised," Bob recounted, "on what might be considered either the brink or the horizon, according to one's point of view, of a successful Hollywood career."

Bob's contacts in the First Motion Picture Unit at Culver City were paying off handsomely, and he had more appointments for screen tests, interviews with agents and producers, and lunch dates than he knew how to handle. One day he was driving down Sunset Boulevard with James Hilton on the way to an appointment at Paramount Studios. He was describing to Hilton the role Paramount wanted him to take when the writer stopped him short.

"You can stay here in Hollywood, and I'm sure you'll make a success of it," he said. "You'll probably become a star of sorts, but Hollywood is going to absorb you, you know that. As long as you stay here you're going to be just another actor. What you were doing at Barter Theatre was important—not just to you, but to the actors you gave jobs to and the people you played to. If it were my choice, I'd want my name to be associated with Barter Theatre, not with Hollywood."

Hilton, Bob knew, spoke out of his deep love for the theatre and, Bob realized, Hilton's affection for him. "What he said touched my conscience," said Bob. "I wasn't living up to what I could and should be doing, and I knew it. What was worse, I wasn't getting the joy theatre had once given me."

He decided to at least visit his family in Virginia while he thought over what Hilton had said. He also wanted to see if the tornado damage was as bad as he remembered.

It was worse.

Alice Hilton accepts barter for tickets, circa 1947.

Bob with Mrs. Eleanor Roosevelt.

Bob with President Harry Truman. They were great admirers of each other.

The buildings were little more than gaunt shells—the porches gone and the trees and shrubbery uprooted and dead. Piles of debris still lay scattered about, and the collapsed wall had been so shoddily rebuilt that it looked as if it might collapse again with the slightest breeze. All of the furniture that had not been destroyed by the storm had been given to Emory & Henry College, and the property was once again up for sale at an asking price of fifteen thou-

sand dollars per dormitory. Even if Bob could secure its use to
restart Barter Theatre, the physical plant could be sold out from
under him at any second.

Bob wondered if the gesture of renouncing Hollywood would
end up being noble or patently foolish. Perhaps Barter Theatre had
outgrown its original function of providing jobs for hungry actors?
Even though he considered them far lesser artistically than live theatre, he knew that movies and radio were now supplying plenty of
cheap or free entertainment even in the hinterlands of Virginia. He
also knew that television's arrival in Southwest Virginia was only a
matter of time.

Actors were no longer in danger of going hungry during the season of 1945–46; Broadway was booming. The barter economy that
had helped people make it through the Great Depression seemed to
be and was for the most part a thing of the past. The easy decision
would be to tell himself that he had accomplished what he had set
out to do. He had survived the lean years and had provided jobs
and three square meals a day to hundreds of actors, he had brought
live theatre into the Bible Belt, and he had overcome many of the
prejudices rural people held against the theatre. Wasn't that enough
of an accomplishment for any man? He knew that he could easily
argue that it was.

He had started with nothing on what by then seemed like a youthful lark, and here he was thirteen years less youthful and without
Fritz at his side, kicking at the rubble of what had once been his
dream and his life. He closed his eyes for a moment, remembering;
then he made his decision: he would go back to Hollywood.

On the day before he had airline reservations to fly west to California, Bob was standing in front of the Abingdon courthouse talking to a couple of local businessmen who had supported his earlier
efforts at bringing theatre to Abingdon. Then an elderly African
American lady who had been one of Barter Theatre's regular mati-
nee patrons came up to greet Bob and shake his hand.

"'Was I going to bring back my show people?'" Bob remembered
that she asked. He stood for a moment, holding her weathered and
cracked black hands between his large white ones. Even though
segregation was an "accepted" way of life throughout the South in

those days, one thing Bob Porterfield had always insisted upon was that there would be no segregation in his theatre, either for the audience or in the companies. In his eyes, everyone was God's child regardless of race or circumstance. Not wanting to destroy her enthusiasm and huge smile, he said nothing. The businessmen's eyes went from one face to the other.

"I just wanted you to know," she said, "I'm fixing to plant a garden pretty soon, and I was going to put in an extra row of beans if you're going to be back."

In the years to come, Robert Huffard Porterfield sometimes wondered what might have happened if he had boarded that airplane back to Hollywood.

— 12 —

Welcome Back!

One hundred and thirty-four of Barter's former actors had served in the war, in all branches of the military. Four had won Distinguished Service Crosses, but only two had failed to make it home. With the exception of one or two who had put on plays and skits for their fellow soldiers, they had not been on the stage for up to five years, and all were burning with a desire to return to the theatre. Many had met kindred spirits along the way and wanted to introduce them to Bob and Barter Theatre. Old-timers such as Larry Gates, Owen Phillips, Mell Turner, Herbert Nelson, Fred Stewart, Elizabeth Wilson, and Betty Moore soon visited Bob, who had set up a casting shop of sorts in the apartment of his old friend Bob Pastene above the Hudson Theatre in New York.

The old-timers especially came full of happy memories and dreams of what Barter Theatre might become in the future. The younger actors arrived lured by Bob Porterfield's reputation as a man willing to give untried performers a chance. That year he interviewed more than 750 applicants before settling on the 75 or so whom he liked best.

Eighteen were Equity members hired at Equity's standard salary for summer theatre. Others came for their room and board and the love of theatre, and still others came as apprentices who paid cash for their own room and board in exchange for the opportunity to be part of a professional theatrical company.

Bob knew that Fritz would not be coming back to help him resume his dream, but although his brain knew this to be the truth, his soul refused to accept it. Several times he caught himself on the verge of referring some problem or the other to her, then quickly stopped himself. Bob's aunt, Miss Elizabeth Huffard, had thrown her energy into making one of the dormitories of the old Stonewall Jackson Institute habitable, but even with her best efforts the place looked bleak. The soft beds that had been loaned to the navy training program at Emory & Henry College during Bob's absence never found their way back, but army surplus cots and triple-decker bunks were found to replace them, which also had the advantage of making it easier to pack more actors in each room. After some buckets of cheap paint and a few posters were applied to the walls, the dormitory once again christened the Barter Inn was still spartan at best, but at least it had a roof that was more or less waterproof.

Enthusiasm was high that spring, but as usual the cash supply was low as Bob set out to pick up the shards of a theatre shattered by a world war and a tornado. However, he remembered that in 1941 the Commonwealth of Virginia had designated Barter as the official State Theatre of Virginia, the first state to ever bestow such a designation, and the Virginia legislature had promised a cash grant of ten thousand dollars. The money had never been appropriated, but Bob decided he had to travel to Richmond to see if there was still any chance of collecting the promised funds.

Accompanied by several prominent businessmen from Abingdon and the western end of Virginia who saw the recognition and economic benefits that Barter Theatre could bring to the area, Bob argued his case before politicians and bureaucrats that Virginia's natural beauty brought in money-spending tourists, and that even more would come if there were cultural activities as well, or, as he put it, a little "after dark" entertainment.

Virginians have always prided themselves on their culture, he told the assembled legislators. After all, he said, the first theatre in America was built in Williamsburg in 1712, and even before that the earliest-known acting company in the new world, consisting of Cornelius Atkinson, Phillip Howard, and William Darby, presented a play, *Ye Bare and Ye Cub*, on August 27, 1665, at Thomas Fowkes's Tavern in what would become Accomack County. Never mind that the little troupe was dragged into His Majesty's Court by an offended

Bob and Barter were back in business after the war. Even though American tastes had changed and the economy had improved, there was still a demand for live theatre in the Virginia mountains.

citizen named Edward Martin who ended up losing his case and being ordered to pay court costs.

To the delight of Bob and his supporters, his oratory won the day. Virginia, in 1946, again made history by giving the theatre a grant of ten thousand dollars and the promise of more funds in subsequent years. Bob always felt that the grant money was channeled through an appropriate medium, the budget of the Department of Conservation and Development—right along with funds for preserving Virginia's forests, parks, and wildlife.

Bob's theatre—which had now become Virginia's theatre as well—began its first postwar season, naturally enough, by running counter to the trend of other stock companies. Many of the old and distinguished summer theatres had gone out of business permanently during the war, and the new ones opening up to take their places made no pretense of being anything other than money-making enterprises, even if some of them were technically not-for-profit. A commercially successful concept known as the "package star system" was gaining widespread acceptance. Producers would recruit one widely known national star—such as, for example, Tallulah Bankhead—whom the public would pay high ticket prices to see, then put together a complete touring package complete with a few additional actors and a publicity man or two, props, sets, costumes, and sometimes even lights. They then offered local theatres in what they somewhat derisibly called the "Straw Hat Circuit" the whole enterprise for a fixed percentage of the box office receipts. To preserve the illusion of "local" theatre, the touring operation would rehearse for a few days with members of the local theatre's company appearing in bit parts, carrying spears or making up the chorus.

Bob disliked this system for many reasons. First, it virtually destroyed the idea of local professional companies; also, the producers and the star left town with most of the money. But more damaging than either of these, Bob believed, such packaged products gave small-town audiences neither the genuine excitement of Broadway nor the joy and spontaneity of small and dedicated companies of unknown professionals plying the trade they loved. The shows, though slickly and too perfectly done, simply had little if any heart and offered the satisfaction of assembly-line-produced, store-bought cakes. He much preferred the old-style ensemble repertory company, a group of relatively unknown but highly talented and motivated actors and other theatre professionals who worked together through a number of productions, often several at once and sometimes even over several years. Bob always liked to say that playing repertory is the best known way to "cure young hams," and he truly believed it.

The 1946 Barter Theatre staff was divided into two companies: the red company and the white company. One would play in Abingdon while the other toured to nearby towns in Virginia, Tennessee,

Kentucky, and North Carolina; then, at midweek, the companies would switch places. While presenting one show every evening, each company would be rehearsing the next two shows, effectively keeping up to a dozen plays in regular rotation so that citizens of Abingdon and tourists could see two, three, or sometimes even four plays in a given week. Bob obviously wanted his hams well-cured.

One young man who braved the grueling schedule hitchhiked into Abingdon one morning and told Bob that he was originally from Connecticut, had been in the regular navy for the past ten years, and needed work. He wasn't asking for an acting job, he insisted, although he did admit that he had caught the acting bug and had spent a couple of months at an acting school. What he wanted was just a job of any sort connected with the theatre and which paid room and board.

Bob instinctively liked something about the young man, perhaps the fact that he was big and burly, always a handy sort of person to have around when heavy sets have to be moved, and he said he could drive a truck. He ended up staying around for five years. The companies began to rely on him both in Abingdon and on tour.

On the tailgate of one of Barter's trucks salvaged from prewar days was the brush-painted legend "Gregory Peck drove this truck." The ex-sailor with his trademark gap-toothed smile loved to drive that truck especially. When he was behind its wheel, he always said, he knew that the truck was lucky and that it would help him to someday get ahead in show business.

> There was something about the boy—his virility and vitality, his great warmth and dynamic personality—that made you like him instantly. He made friends easily and had that rugged "diamond in the rough" aspect. He played a few walk-ons during the course of that first summer, and I could see that he had an instant rapport with the audience.
>
> I got a hunch about him and wrote myself a letter, as I sometimes do, to be opened ten years later. I predicted that he would hit the top of the profession. It was something under the ten-year deadline that I opened the letter to myself and read it—on the occasion of the boy's first Oscar, awarded for his title role as Marty Pilletti in *Marty*.

Ernie Borgnine accepts his Oscar for best actor from Grace Kelly. Ernie hitchhiked into Abingdon one day, and Bob hired him to drive trucks, move heavy sets, and act a little. Bob said he knew from the start there was "something special about the boy." Nine years later, Ernie won his Oscar.

The hitchhiker hired and given a chance by Bob Porterfield was born Ermes Effron Borgnino, but America came to love him as Ernest Borgnine. Many years later, Borgnine would remember Bob Porterfield: "He gave me my start in the business, and every time I see my Oscar, I remember him fondly."

Nineteen-forty-six also saw the revival of the annual Barter Awards in New York. The honoree that year was Louis Calhern, who had produced *The Magnificent Yankee*, a play about Chief Justice Oliver Wendell Holmes. Tallulah Bankhead was also there to

Bob presents a Virginia ham to David Merrick, Broadway producer.

accept her 1943 Barter Award, the presentation of which had been delayed by the war.

Tallulah and Bob, both southerners by birth and rebels by inclination, laughingly challenged one another to get through the entire evening without once uttering the word "Yankee." They toasted and complimented Calhern's "magnificent play," but deftly danced around actually saying the complete title. It wasn't long before the other guests caught on to Tallulah and Bob's little joke and began hanging on every word, waiting for one of them to slip up. Dorothy Stickney finally presented the hams, and Bob presented deeds to the acres of mountain land, but not once during the luncheon did he or Tallulah slip.

The 1946 cast and crew could have lodged rent-free in the old dormitory of the Stonewall Jackson property, still vacant and unsold as it was, but Bob knew the time had come—if it was ever going to—for Barter Theatre to plant its roots deep in the Virginia soil with a permanent home. He had enough money saved from his *Sergeant York* and *The Yearling* paychecks to put a down payment on one of the dorms. Kalita Humphreys and Monty Hare, Barter's new resident playwright, chipped in with Alice Hilton, who had come to Abingdon to join Barter's company, to carry the second mortgage. Bob now had his choice of either dormitory for fifteen thousand dollars. He chose the one with the reconstructed wall because it had a finished attic for costume storage and a more complete basement. The ink had hardly dried on the bill of sale before the troupe moved in.

Nearly four years is a long time to be away, and Bob wondered apprehensively if the audiences he had only begun to train to share his love of the theatre would welcome the company back. The years between 1943 and 1946 had been hard ones for almost everybody. Even in Virginia the old way of life was passing. Tractors had almost completely replaced draft horses and mules; most rural families now had a telephone and electric lights, and most owned a radio. Freed from wartime production needs and material shortages, factories had begun cranking out consumer products such as refrigerators and electric ranges by the trainload, and Detroit seemed bound and determined to put everybody in America behind the wheel. Would Abingdon and Southwest Virginia, Bob wondered, still embrace his idea of live theatre? Would people be willing to pay the $1.20 per ticket that Bob calculated he needed to meet the payroll? To cushion the shock of the price increase, patrons could buy a season ticket book good for ten plays for $6 that cut the cost per ticket down to 60 cents, but that was still a long way from milking oneself a ticket or trading a tub of homemade cottage cheese to see *Smilin' Thru.*

"Colonel" John Sage, the caretaker who more or less came with Barter's newly acquired property, greeted Bob heartily and introduced him to his youngest son, whom he had named "Robert" in Bob's honor. The people of Abingdon and the surrounding countryside welcomed Bob and his troupe as if they were long-lost friends from before the terrible war. They also gave more than just lip service to their southern hospitality. Did Bob need furniture? Costumes? What about fabrics?

Soon the Barter Inn began to fill up with used chairs, second-hand chests-of-drawers, and tables. Abingdon reeked of mothballs as people all over town dug into trunks and boxes to come up with every kind of costume imaginable from hoop-skirted gowns to military uniforms to wedding dresses. It wasn't long before Bob had a wardrobe with more and better outfits than before the tornado. Rolls and boxes of fabrics—brocades, monk's cloth, black jet, damasks, and velveteens—also came in. Even old draperies arrived ready to be cut and sewn into cloaks and capes.

J. J. Cozart, who owned numerous large tobacco warehouses in the area, put at Bob's disposal Warehouse #1 to serve for the summer as a scene shop. The huge warehouse, used in the fall and winter for tobacco auctions, enclosed more than four football fields worth of space. In addition to having far more than enough room in which to build sets, the warehouse had good lighting from its many skylights and was infused with the warm, comfortable smell of mellow barn-cured Virginia burley.

With the purchase of its own property Barter Theatre was no longer viewed as a fly-by-night outfit but as a real business entity. Southwest Virginia and Abingdon—now with a population of more than four thousand—began to fill with regional pride over Barter's presence.

"We matched the town's spirit with our own," remembered Bob.

> All of us had been for three or more years suspended from the world which was the only real world to us—the theatre. We had been bottling up our dreams and passions for the stage all this time, and now we were able to unleash them on a scale beyond our dreams. V-E Day and V-J Day had released us to pursue our art more intently, more patriotically, more devotedly than ever. Absent so long from the stage and from the audience, we were passionately determined to prove to the world and to ourselves that we could still act, direct, design, and make a world of magic.

As America's first state theatre, everyone involved with Barter felt upon them the eyes of the entire theatre world and of state legislatures throughout the country, intently watching to see if Bob Porterfield and his people proved that regional professional repertory theatres could survive far from major cities.

One of the actors who was there that summer later commented,

"Every actor that summer played every part as though the fate of theatre in America rested upon his shoulders, and the same spirit pervaded every production and every member of the company, down to the apprentices who swept out the stage and picked up bobby pins on the dressing room floor."

None of Barter's offerings in 1946 included a known "star," but several people out of the troupe went on to successful careers in theatre and Hollywood, including, of course, Ernest Borgnine. There was only a group of hard-working actors who were awakened each morning with a ringing cowbell. They were, Bob said later, "in love with the audience, and they had glamour in their souls."

Not everyone in Southwest Virginia welcomed Bob and his players, but even those who did not often made an unintentional contribution as well. The Reverend Dan Graham, older now but still a self-appointed thorn in Barter's side, was one example. Freed from the uniformity demanded by the war, several of Bob's male actors were the first men to ever appear on Abingdon's Main Street in Bermuda shorts, and the actresses sometimes showed up in shorts and halter outfits that were, Bob admitted, "rather abbreviated."

The next thing anybody knew, the right good Reverend Graham was going all over town taking up a collection of clothes for "that nudist colony" up at Barter. He delivered the clothing collection to Bob with "a prayer for the salvation of [his] soul." Ever the gentleman, Bob accepted the clothing and the prayer with good grace and later commented that both "have worn pretty well."

Miss Ethel Baugh, whose little business, the Goods and Chattels Shop, had so often given or loaned props and costumes to Barter Theatre from its very first production, was ailing that summer, and she expressed to Bob how sorry she was not to be able to see Barter's plays as she had always done before. She said she especially missed being able to see *The Happy Journey*, which she had been told was one of the loveliest plays ever. On the afternoon of her seventh-third birthday, Barter's players gave a command performance of the play on her back porch, and she was able to watch it from her bed.

Virginia's governor, William Tuck, came to Barter in late July, accompanied by a sizable entourage. His purpose, other than seeing

Arms and the Man, was to lay the cornerstone for a planned annex to the theatre. The only problem was that ground had not even been broken yet, and there actually was no cornerstone to lay.

"A minor detail," Bob assured Governor Tuck. He took a small metal fishing tackle box, filled it with mementos such as a string of beads from Helen Hayes, one of Gregory Peck's pipes, and Laurette

Bob hams it up with Barter Company member Anne Ives.

Taylor's "spangled pants." The governor then, between acts, happily and ceremoniously "laid" it just off the apron of the stage. The box and its contents was later embedded in the real cornerstone.

"This business of laying a cornerstone when there wasn't even a foundation seems to sum up in a nutshell most of my brainstorms and the whole history of Barter Theatre," said Bob.

> We were always going ahead and doing things and laying our plans on faith, and eventually somebody nearly always came along behind us and dug the foundation we had been taking for granted all along. It wasn't rational or practical, but it was certainly theatrical. The cornerstone that wasn't seemed to symbolize our whole history of doing first and asking after. Thank goodness Saint Rita was not among the casualties of the tornado.

Everywhere he went, Bob still kept in his pocket the little Patron Saint of the Impossible to keep her warm.

13

You Saved My Life

With both the Great Depression and World War II receding into history and the memories of graying Americans, life seemed to take on a hectic pace similar to the expansionism and belief in manifest destiny that had characterized the country following the War Between the States. New cars, many of them brightly colored as if in defiance of tradition, almost overnight filled streets and highways. The hammering of carpenters building new houses made a symphony of progress, and thousands of eager veterans headed to trade schools and colleges under the G.I. Bill. Hospital pediatric wards became nearly swamped with the arrival of hundreds of babies.

Despite movies in color, hundreds of new radio stations, and television, America wanted live theatre as never before, not just in New York but even in the remotest of rural villages.

Barter Theatre had always toured its shows to spread theatre as far afield as Bob could afford the gasoline for his trucks and buses. The company played Bristol, with its distinction of a State Street center stripe that is the border between Virginia and Tennessee. It played Marion, where the company had to lug their sets and equipment up three flights of stairs to a little auditorium in the county courthouse. It played Rural Retreat, known as the cabbage capital of the world and hometown of Dr Pepper. It played Saltville, Damascus, Rye Cove, Mendota, and seemingly every little wide spot in the roads between.

There were adventures, but with tenacity and good luck most of them turned out for the better, even though Bob still had to constantly keep his eye on both the condition of his battered trucks and buses and on what had been Fritz's little tin money box.

Gate City, Virginia, about fifty-four miles from Abingdon, was one of the most distant towns in which Barter regularly played. One afternoon Bob and the company had just about finished getting up their scenery in the Gate City school's gymnasium when something caused the electricity to go out—and stay out—all over town. The company held an emergency meeting and discovered that by combining all the cash everyone had, their resources amounted to two dollars and a few pennies, and the gas tanks of both the truck and bus were empty.

Luckily, the town's hardware store was still open, so Bob gave the troupe's last two dollars to the prop girl and told her to go and buy as many candles as she could. The rest of the company went out swinging an old cow bell through the streets and shouting, "Come and see the flesh-and-blood Barter Theatre! We've got our own lights!"

At just before curtain time they placed the candles on borrowed saucers across the stage. Bob later recalled, "I remember thinking how pretty the girls looked by candlelight." He also knew that fifty-four miles was going to be a long way for more than twenty people to hitchhike back to Abingdon in the middle of the night.

"Then we saw them coming, the length of the town, swinging their lanterns in front of them, bringing their chickens and eggs and potatoes and watercress," said Bob. "Enough of them brought cash, as I discovered when I counted up the night's take, for us to buy enough gasoline to get home on."

This was all a far cry from cruising Sunset Boulevard in a new convertible with the top down, but Barter's appearances in remote Appalachian communities sometimes led to things far more exciting. One evening the troupe played *Cradle Song* in Big Stone Gap, Virginia, in an empty armory where there were no dressing room facilities, so the women had to leave on their costumes—black nun's habits—for the bus ride back to Abingdon. Everything was going along just fine until "Bessie the Bus" broke down and drifted to a stop from which she refused to budge. Everybody stepped off the bus to see what was wrong with her this time, and several nearby farmers attracted by the noise hurried out to see if they could help. They took one look, though, at the dark array of girls dressed in long black dresses with black hoods and white collars shining in the lights of their lanterns and immediately hightailed it in a frightened run.

The little towns the companies played knew show business only by the radio or the two-dimensional entertainment of the movies, and live theatre brought into the hollows and valleys the breath of a different world. A little girl from one mountain hamlet was so awe-struck by the spectacle of a live show unfolding before her eyes that she climbed up onto the stage and began following Hume Cronyn around. At last she found the courage to reach out and touch him. "Look, Mama!" she exclaimed in delight. "These are round actors!"

Another time, the players took a lighthearted Kaufman and Hart comedy to the town of Coeburn. It was Barter's first appearance in the little town, and everyone was anxious to make a good first impression. The auditorium was filled to standing room only, which made Bob confident of success. The show had been a huge hit on Broadway and in Abingdon.

During the first act, however, even though the jokes and sight gags flew thick and fast, there was not a sound out of the audience. The actors, who had at first been relaxed, began playing harder and harder, emphasizing their laugh lines, mugging, hamming, and falling into all the tricks of bad actors and broad playing just to get any sort of audience reaction. During intermission the actors asked Bob to go out into the audience and assure them that there were actually real people out there beyond the footlights. They were real, all right, and every one of them hurried back to his or her seat after the intermission. At least nobody had gone home. All during the second act the company played harder than ever, but the best punch lines and rowdiest slapstick couldn't even draw a giggle. Bob said, "It was worse than playing for radio."

Somehow everyone got through the play and went to the dressing rooms to take off their makeup, exhausted and depressed. There was a delegation of townspeople waiting for them when they emerged. "I had an awful stab of panic," Bob said,

wondering if they had come to ride us out of town on a rail. Had
we really been that bad? But they were beaming. Gratification
and appreciation were written all over their faces. "Boy, your
show sure was good," they kept repeating, while we stood there
dumbfounded. "Boy, Howdy, that really was some good play!"
Finally one old fellow could contain himself no longer. "Yessir,"
he said, rubbing his hands together. "That show of yours was so
funny we couldn't hardly keep from laughing!"

Bob continued to believe that his Barter Theatre could and should
make a difference not just in Southwest Virginia, but throughout
the country. He believed it could sow the seeds of professional regional theatre wherever it went, and he put his beliefs into action
by assembling two touring companies for the autumn of 1946 and
spring of 1947. These tours, Bob realized, would be far different
from the trips of the summer. For one thing they would often be
playing in larger towns where people had seen plays, even seen
them on Broadway, and were not to be impressed by the sheer novelty of live theatre.

He also knew that touring is anything but carefree when one has
to deal with enough scenery, props, and costumes to stage seven
plays, usually on one-night stands. The salaried company, originally planned to consist of twenty-four people, had somehow grown
to thirty-five. All of the principal actors were under Equity contract, and Bob was obligated to each of them for a minimum weekly
salary of sixty dollars plus their room and board. Others such as
Ernie Borgnine, who doubled as drivers, stagehands, and extras,
drew little more than the cost of their room and board, but even
that was substantial.

Bob had contracted with a booking agent to line up performance
dates and sponsors, but few of the sponsors were willing to promise the companies a minimum for their appearances; they would
have to play for whatever could be taken in at the box office. At least,
Bob decided, the touring companies would accept only cash in payment since operating mobile commissaries would be impossible.

On a morning in September with the warm smell of burning
leaves in the air, the companies loaded up their two specially constructed trucks with the assorted scenery, costumes, light bridges,

platforms, sound boxes, and chandeliers. Somebody calculated that if all the cargo of the two trucks had been combined, they could have furnished a ten-room house, clothed an army of almost any era, opened two dress shops, or rigged a ten-masted schooner. When everything was squeezed onto the trucks, Bob wished the members of his company Godspeed as they climbed onto the buses.

As the caravan rumbled down the street and out of sight, Bob stood for several minutes, his mind awash with all that had happened, with all that would happen. His acting companies were for him like the children whom he desperately wanted but had never had, and now they were going out into the big, wide world without him.

> I would have liked to have gone with them, of course. Acting was my first love in the theatre, and the audience my second; it was what I had been trained for, certainly not for the involved business of being an accountant, impresario, talent scout, tightwad and drummer rolled into one—in other words, a producer. But I had committed myself to making a go of a year-round state theatre of Virginia, and I found out that called for a full-time manager at the helm, namely me. The theatre's assorted real estate demanded a caretaker, especially since we had taken paying guests at Barter Inn to cover the yearly cost of upkeep, servants, heat, and utilities. The money I could make in occasional speaking engagements would come in handy in tiding us over a rainy week. And the office detail of guiding destinies of two touring companies in a repertory of seven plays was a full-time job in itself. There is a reason the old-time actor-managers have had their day; running a theatre has grown in complexity and difficulty until it absorbs the full capacity of any man. And I had another reason for staying in Abingdon; I had added to the job of the theatre another profession equally precarious, and taken over the management of the family farm, Twin Oaks, with its herd of sixty dairy cows.

Bob managed to catch the performances of his companies many times and places, but it was never the same as actually being a participant. A few members tried at first to keep diaries for him to read

later, but in the press of eighteen-hour days these soon tapered off
to nothing, though he was told the stories of their adventures. There
was the time the bus grew so cold that the ink froze inside their
fountain pens, and in Roaring Gap, North Carolina, they played on
a floating waterfront stage designed for concerts, not theatre. To get
from stage right to stage left, the actors had to get into a little boat
behind the backdrop and row forty feet. One night one of the actresses missed her mark and fell into the lake. And there was the time
that the truck driver, who couldn't read, turned east instead of west
on Highway 229 and ended up 250 miles away from where the actors who had arrived on the buses had to present their play by
lantern light with no costumes, no scenery, and no props. There
was the eighteen-hole golf course at one hotel, the bedbugs in another, an 8 a.m. performance in Paris, Tennessee, co-ed dressing
rooms, and the almost constant stench of gymnasiums.

The outstanding recollection shared by them all, Bob said, was
that they were wanted. It was a great year to go on tour because the
recently ended war had shifted people's lives upside down and con-
fined them with gasoline rationing, and now they were eager for
the gregarious experience of going to see live theatre.

Theatre people often speak of places as being "good theatre
towns" where actors are welcomed and the standards they are held
to are high. Philadelphia, New Haven, and Toronto, all large cities
with a core of people who know and appreciate good plays and good
actors, are known as good theatre towns. Eighty-three of the 112
towns played by a Barter company that season, however, were in
Virginia, and the Commonwealth at that time had only 53 towns
larger than twenty-five hundred population. It was exciting to discover that even small communities such as Natural Bridge and Lees-
burg and Tappahannock-on-the-Rappahannock were also good theatre towns. So were Hazard, Kentucky, and Independence, Virginia.

There was no effort to tailor the repertory for small-town audiences, to try to pick "easy to understand" plays for people not used
to theatre or who had limited education. Bob just selected the seven
best shows he could find. One company toured *Arms and the Man*,
Blithe Spirit, and *Virginia Overture*; the other toured *State of the Union*
and *Our Town*. Each company had everything it needed, including

its own truck, bus, lighting equipment, stage manager, and company manager, but the two companies occasionally combined their efforts for that season's two biggest productions: *Wings over Europe* and *Much Ado about Nothing*.

Shakespeare, in fact, turned out to attract bigger audiences than anything else the companies did, and if they ever worried about playing in small towns, they could always look back on War, West Virginia. A reporter from *Billboard* magazine had talked his way into being allowed to go along for a week to do a story about theatre's reception in small and out-of-the-way corners of the hinterlands. He joined up with the company at Clifton Forge, Virginia, but when told that the next stop was to be the tiny coal mining town of War, West Virginia, he practically hooted. "Was there any possibility," he wanted to know, "any possibility at all that an audience of coal miners would understand, much less appreciate a snappy and brittle comedy such as Noel Coward's *Blithe Spirit*?"

The company had been asked to schedule an early-evening curtain time so the miners could still get a good night's sleep and be ready to descend into their shafts before daylight the following morning. As curtain time drew near, men seemed to be coming directly from the mines, wearing their grubby work clothes, carrying their empty dinner pails, and with some wearing their helmets with the carbide-burning headlights still attached. Their faces appeared grim and black, hidden behind a thick layer of coal dust with only their eyes and lips visible. Sneaking glances around the curtain as the auditorium filled to capacity, the company began to share the city reporter's skepticism. To all of their amazements, especially that of the reporter, *Blithe Spirit* played that evening to one of the most appreciative audiences it had ever seen, and nobody tried "not to laugh." Put War, West Virginia, down, Bob said, as a "good theatre town."

By the time the two companies returned to Abingdon in the spring of 1947, they had played 353 performances in 112 communities, traveling more than twenty thousand miles by bus over rough roads to perform in six states. More than 141,000 people had bought tickets with cash money, pulling Barter out of the financial hole it had been in at the beginning of September.

In April 1947 Barter once again held its annual awards luncheon at Town Hall in New York City. Bob had no intention of letting Broadway forget what he was doing with regional theatre, pioneering new theatre towns and carrying the banner of Virginia as being the first and, at that time, the only state to lend its support to a state theatre.

Helen Hayes was the honoree that year because she had, in Bob's words, "turned a mediocre play, *Happy Birthday*, into a dazzling showpiece." Among the constellation of stars at the luncheon was Governor William Tuck. Bob had asked him to present the traditional gifts of a ham, a platter, and the deed to an acre of cliffish land to Helen Hayes, and he was delighted. Rotund, happy, and usually the most erudite of men, Governor Tuck became so excited to be presenting the prizes to the beautiful and famous actress that he, probably for the only time in his life, offered a dangling preposition.

"It is my honor to present you with this Virginia ham," Governor Tuck told Miss Hayes, "and here is the platter to eat it off of."

His words instantly became a Barter tradition and have been used ever since. Even today, a playwright whose work is produced at Barter is given a ham, and these words, as part of the royalties.

———

After 1947, recounted Bob, the summers began to pile up one upon another, making it hard to remember each one distinctly, to set all the faces and plays into their proper context. There were a few memorable disasters, such as the time a fire destroyed the entire set, worth more than five thousand dollars, for *East Lynne* at the high school in Kingsport, Tennessee, but memorable successes far outnumbered the disasters. One of the successes was when Mary Chase allowed Barter to stage her runaway Broadway hit *Harvey*, and Brock Pemberton, who had produced the play on the Great White Way, came to Abingdon to play the role of Elwood.

Barter's *Harvey* also seemed to be the big break for Ernie Borgnine. Pemberton liked Ernie's work and offered him employment on Broadway. Borgnine happily accepted, but after a few weeks he decided that he would rather be touring with Barter's company than playing bit parts in New York. He returned to Abingdon and stayed at Barter for three more years.

The fall and winter 1947–48 tour was far more ambitious than anything Bob had attempted to date. It went to twenty-two states and 241 cities and towns, some of them not even on the roadmap, and it racked up 53,610 miles. Sometimes, Bob said, even the bus driver had no idea where they were. One time, the story goes, about 30 miles west of Fort Worth, the bus ran into a blinding blizzard. The troupe tried to keep going because they had a performance scheduled for that evening, but after what seemed like hours without spotting a single road sign, the driver pulled over when he spied a gaunt cow standing beside a little range shack out of which could be discerned the faint glow of a kerosene lamp. With the blue norther howling around him, the driver knocked on the door. When an old rancher finally opened it, the driver admitted that he was lost. "We've been driving for miles without a sign," he said. "Where *are* we?"

The rancher took his time answering. He spat on the ground and hitched up his britches before he spoke. "Texas," he said.

The actors later swore that the cow tried to leave with them on the bus.

Bob found it impossible to join his company for more than a few performances due to their distance from Abingdon and his many responsibilities both at the theatre and on the dairy farm. There was one performance, however, that he would always remember, and that was in Bloomington, Indiana.

The performance's sponsor, a Mr. Riley, had offered the company double the guarantee they normally requested, but he made the offer on the condition that Bob Porterfield come out to Bloomington for the appearance. He paid all of Bob's travel expenses to fly out, and all during the time the company was in town he treated them royally at his expense.

Finally Bob could contain his curiosity no longer. "People have been nice to us before in lots of places," he told Mr. Riley, "but no one has been this nice. There must be some reason, isn't there?"

Mr. Riley smiled. "There is," he said. "You saved my life."

> I have an uncommon good memory for people, and I was sure I had never seen the man before. His reply stumped me, and when I asked how I could possibly have saved his life, he told

me a story. Before the Depression he had been a financier on Wall Street, and in the crash he had lost every nickel he owned. The future looked so bleak that he had been on the verge of jumping out a window—literally. And then, by chance, he picked up a newspaper and an article in it caught his eye. It told about a group of actors, all just about penniless, who had decided to pick up and start all over again. They were going down to a little town in Virginia to see if they could trade their craft for enough to eat on.

"Right then and there," Mr. Riley told me, "I decided that if twenty actors could do it, I could pick up and start all over again too." He did not have to finish the story with a punch line—I knew the ending already. He had become president of Indiana Limestone.

14

Something Barter in Denmark

It seemed that for the next few years Bob and the Barter Theatre were riding waves of success. Money was always a problem, as it seems to be perpetually for regional theatres, but Barter's reputation and Bob's hard work were beginning to attract more and more private and corporate donors, well aware of the economic benefits accruing to Abingdon and Southwest Virginia from the increasingly famous theatre.

On the evening of Easter Sunday 1948, Bob was in New York to be presented with a Tony Award for his "Contribution to the Development of Regional Theatre." The Tony Awards honor actress Antoinette Perry, who died in 1946 and who, Bob always believed, literally worked herself to death trying to help actors during the Great Depression and supporting America during the war. The award is given annually to people who have been most outstanding during the Broadway theatrical season. It was traditionally and for many years awarded only to people involved directly with Broadway productions, but the award's board of directors voted unanimously to honor Bob for his pioneering efforts in regional theatre. The Tony was so new at the time that there was no official trophy. Instead, the men were given a gold money clip, and the ladies were presented with a golden bracelet. All received a scroll of recognition.

"Tribute is sweet," said Bob,

> especially when it brings a spotlight to bear on the crusade you have been waging most of your life. Ever since I left Broadway behind I have been fighting to make regional theatre its equal in quality and in honor. The Tony seemed to bring it a step closer,

and I thought of Antoinette Perry, the sympathetic heart who had responded to my appeal to the Stage Relief Committee sixteen years gone by like a thrifty housewife, donating curtains and scenery to my struggling brainstorms. I like to think she would have been pleased.

In the stormy battleground of the Bible Belt, Bob knew that he had picked a most unlikely place for his battle to gain acceptance for a theatre. One of the very first gifts Barter Theatre ever received was during that first summer of 1933. It came from Rabbi Kalish of Richmond and was a five-dollar bill with a note attached. The note read: "Understand you are starting a theatrical company in the Bible Belt of Virginia. I think you need help."

I didn't realize how far we had come until the spring of 1948, not long after the Tony presentation. That was when I received another award, from a far different and entirely unexpected source—my old alma mater, Hampden-Sydney College. The college I never graduated from awarded me the honorary degree of Doctor of Letters for my work in the theatre, and I became a June graduate at last. Colgate Darden, president of the University of Virginia [who spoke at the ceremony], feigned amazement. "What is this staid old Presbyterian college coming to?" he exclaimed. "Ten years ago this couldn't have happened—granting degrees for anything so wicked as work in the theatre!"

Bob considered his honorary degree a major breakthrough in his life and the life of his theatre. By winning stature in the academic world and even a degree of acceptance by religious leaders, he felt that he was at last winning his battle with old prejudices and making the stage respectable even in the Bible Belt.

"I don't think I've seen an acting group anywhere since that could top Barter's 1948 company," said Bob. He continued:

Some years later a Hollywood producer who'd had occasion to hire quite a few Barter troupers asked me what gave them so much poise. "Bad stages," I replied. They played on the road under conditions ranging from mediocre to terrible, on stages ranging in size from pocket handkerchiefs to drafty barns, and

they learned how to project in ballrooms, lunchrooms, and court-
yards; how to seek out spotlights instinctively, wherever they
were; how to generate energy when they'd been traveling eighteen hours without a break and carrying scenery up four flights
of stairs.

Bob was proud that the continuity of ensemble playing gave his
group of professional actors the opportunity that is more common
in Europe—steady paid employment over several seasons and the
chance to play a wide and varied range of roles. A top Broadway
actor might work a few weeks—or if he happens to be in a long-
running show, several months—but always in the same role night
after night. In repertory, by contrast, an actor might play six nights
a week in as many different shows ranging from modern comedy to
Shakespeare.

To celebrate Barter's two hundredth production, Bob chose to
stage *Hamlet*. Although Shakespeare's plays seldom break even financially, much less turn a profit, this final offering of the 1948
season turned out at least to be a critical success in Abingdon,
throughout Virginia, and in the dozen or so other states where it
toured. What really set it apart was that it garnered Barter an invitation from the country of Denmark to play *Hamlet* at Elsinore Castle, the first American theatre company ever to be invited there.

According to Bob, when Dave Goodman, the town manager of
Abingdon, learned about the upcoming trip, he jokingly told Bob,
"Now something really *will* be rotten in the State of Denmark!"

Unfortunately, Goodman turned out to be at least partially right,
but the fault lay not with Barter but with the stars, along with outside meddling, those financing the trip, and the bureaucracy in general. As presented by Barter's company, *Hamlet* was, according to
Bob, "excellent. I may even brag a little and say it was superb," but
by the time that a number of cooks had added salt, yanked out
some ingredients, and added others, the resulting presentation retained little of its original excellence.

Sponsored jointly by the U.S. State Department, the government of Denmark, the International Cultural Exchange Branch of
the American National Theatre and Academy (ANTA), and a mil-
lionaire arts angel named Blevins Davis, the play was to be directed

by Bob Breen as it had been in the United States. Breen was also in the lead role, a lifelong dream of his to both direct and star in what many consider Shakespeare's finest play. By all accounts, he did the tortured prince good justice.

Bob Porterfield later said he had assumed Barter would send its original production intact to Denmark, but then things began to change. For openers, Bob Breen went to Bob and told him that the State Department insisted on featuring "name" stars in the main roles to give the tour what it referred to as "prestige."

Somewhat reluctantly but aware of the honor and publicity that playing *Hamlet* in Denmark would bring his theatre, Bob accepted Breen at his word and agreed to the changes. Breen, who apparently did not feel that he, himself, needed to be replaced by a better-known star, immediately went to New York and managed to sign up Clarence Derwent as Polonius, Walter Abel as Claudius, Ruth Ford as Ophelia, and Aline MacMahon as Gertrude. These were all second-tier "stars," at best, but Breen was unable to recruit the top-ranking names he wanted because, as Bob Porterfield learned later, "None of them wanted to be associated with a production in which Hamlet was played by a relatively minor actor."

> When the new members of the cast arrived in Abingdon that May to rehearse, I saw immediately that the ensemble playing, the esprit de corps that had been our hallmark, had gone out the window. The rhythm of playing, the unity of the production, was shot. The new stars, all distinguished individuals, were badly matched. Aline MacMahon was too old to play Gertrude. Clarence Derwent was one of the sweetest men in the theatre I have ever known, but he was no actor. I guess the change that hurt me most was to see Gerry Jedd, [who was] replaced by Ruth Ford in the role of Ophelia, reduced to a walk-on. "Her Ophelia can't touch yours," I told Gerry the day they left for Denmark, "and one day Bob Breen is going to know it."
>
> In the end I stepped out of the picture altogether, unhappy at the patchwork production which was to represent us at Elsinore, yet unwilling to obstruct the smooth operation of such an important pilot project. I knew feuds and explosions of theatrical temperament were the last thing anybody needed. Rather than

making the trip to Denmark, I decided to stay in Abingdon to open Barter's seventeenth season and, with a sinking heart, I went to the Tri-City Airport to see the company loaded into an army transport plane.

"Maybe," Bob admitted, "I'm playing this scene too heavy. It wasn't a fiasco. The kids in the company had a marvelous time. They loved Denmark, they loved Europe, and I think the people there loved them."

By putting in semi-name performers, Barter had put itself into a category in which it was uncomfortable and in which it did not belong. Although the Danes welcomed the company with open arms and every performance was well-attended, the reviews were tepid or worse. Had Barter been allowed to stage its original cast, Bob always thought, it is very likely that the reviews would have been better but that will never be known. In any case, the State Department saw the enthusiastic welcome with which Europeans greeted American performing arts and began scheduling more of them.

"The State Department heard what they had to say," Bob said. "It began sending more and more of America's performing arts abroad—the National Ballet Theatre, *Porgy and Bess*, Marion Anderson, Helen Hayes in *The Skin of Our Teeth*, and a distinguished succession of offerings that have done more good for the American image abroad than the Marshall Plan or half a dozen monkeys going around the moon in orbits."

Bob's faith in the honesty of those around him was later shaken when he learned the truth about the casting of *Hamlet* and that his old friend had abused his trust. "It was not until much later, after *Hamlet* was history, that I discovered the State Department had never suggested a change in cast," he said. "The demand for 'imported' stars came only from Bob Breen; he had wanted to surround himself with big names."

Although disappointed in how *Hamlet* turned out, Bob continued to forge ahead. In fact, his conviction that a repertory company was the best vehicle for a regional theatre was bolstered by the whole experience. *Hamlet* had been great exposure for Barter, and Bob relished publicity however he could get it. He especially valued word-of-mouth testimonials, as anyone who came to Barter

could attest. Nobody is quite sure when Bob began giving his famous curtain speech that always concluded with "If you like us,
talk about us; and if you don't, just keep your mouth shut!" but it
quickly became a part of the Barter experience that audiences
anticipated almost as much as the plays themselves.

It was also about that time that Bob instituted the tradition of
giving away a pair of hose donated by a local hosiery mill to the "person or persons" who had traveled the greatest distance to attend
Barter for the very first time.

> They come from foreign countries, from Europe and Asia and
> north of the Mason-Dixon line. . . . One night in my curtain speech
> when I was trying to find out who was in the audience from far-
> thest away, a man from Honolulu stood up. I asked him how he
> was enjoying his trip, and if he missed the palm trees, and then
> I asked him if he had brought a lei with him. The woman in the
> seat next to him raised her hand. I've been completely non-
> plussed only about three times in my life, but that time I practi-
> cally fell through the curtain.

At other times Bob benefited from sage advice from sometimes
unlikely sources, and he always maintained that he had never met
a person from whom he couldn't learn something useful. When
Queen Elizabeth II journeyed to Jamestown to take part in Virginia's 350th anniversary celebrations, Bob was invited to be introduced to her. A day or so before he was to leave for the ceremony,
Bob confided to Inez, his African American cook, that "I was still a
country boy at heart and not quite sure how one should behave on
being presented to a queen. To Inez, the answer was simple. 'Laws,
Mr. Porterfield, you just ginny-flex!'"

Bob was always trying to find new ways to promote Barter Theatre, Abingdon, and Southwest Virginia. One of them was the Virginia Highlands Festival. It began in 1948 with a few artists and
performers who assembled on the huge front veranda of the Martha
Washington Inn to demonstrate their talents and some local antiques dealers who offered their wares for sale in the ballroom. Bob
was the force behind the festival's establishment, but he had help
from Charles Castleman Vance who, with his wife Mary Dudley

Vance, operated an antiques shop not far from the Barter Theatre in a building constructed in 1747 that originally served as a tavern on the Wilderness Road. The Vances more or less took care of the antiques side of the festival, and they convinced several other dealers to join in.

By then Alice Hilton had permanently moved to Abingdon and was living in a house whose backyard contained an opening to the cavern out of which the wolves had emerged to attack Daniel Boone and his dogs. In many ways, Alice Hilton filled the void in Bob's business and personal life left by Fritz upon her move back to Pennsylvania. Alice was Bob's close friend and sounding board for his ideas, and she gradually assumed more and more managerial duties. In addition, Alice often provided financial support for the theatre.

15

The Show Must Go On

Staying together as a repertory company, apart from the artistic development it fostered and the quality of plays it allowed Barter to stage, often had the side effect of encouraging romance. Despite grueling schedules of performances and rehearsals, courtships that began on stage and by the script occasionally continued off-stage and led to weddings—sometimes as many as four a year. Most of these relationships developed naturally, but not always, as Bob once explained:

> Sometimes the Barter company gave Cupid a gentle shove. On the *Much Ado about Nothing* tour, I'm told, a few irresponsible actors decided to take a page out of Shakespeare's book. They cooked up an imaginary romance between Virginia Mattis and Charles Dorrand, the stage manager, who had not so much as looked at each other. The men in the bus told Charlie how tired they were getting of hearing Virginia sigh over him, that she could hardly open her mouth without telling them how wonderful she thought Charlie was. The girls asked Virginia why she didn't give Charlie a break—after all, he was really suffering over her, and they were getting worried about his health. At length, after many bumpy roads and one-night stands, the two gave in to popular pressure. They've been happily married ever since.
>
> Courting had its hazards, on stage as well as off. Mell Turner could tell you about one of them. During a rehearsal while he was working on the techniques of an ardent love scene with Phena Darner, he misjudged his approach on the kiss and broke his nose.

Mell was full of excuses—he said the harsh work lights of the rehearsal stage had made him miscalculate his distance; kissing is not usually an occupation pursued in strong lights. At any rate, the nose had to be fixed, and he lost two days off the job. I figured that if it had been an arm or a leg broken in the line of duty, he would have been eligible for Workman's Compensation, and I thought a kiss incurred in the line of duty was no exception. We had a little trouble convincing the Workman's Compensation Board that it wasn't a publicity stunt, but in due time they reviewed the case in all seriousness and awarded Mell forty-seven dollars in damages for an accident on the job.

Of all the romances, the one Abingdon took closest to its heart was the backstage courtship "Beatrice" and "Benedict" were carrying on. I knew the way Herb Nelson felt about Joan DeWeese as soon as I saw them parrying the repartee of Shakespeare's fiery lovers in Much Ado about Nothing, but I must admit that I was a little surprised when Dr. Brook, then minister of the Sinking Spring Presbyterian Church in Abingdon, came up to me after seeing the comedy and told me I was going to have a wedding in the company soon.

The thought had already occurred to me, but I wondered what made him so positive. Dr. Brook was slightly deaf, I knew, because I always gave him a seat farther down front. "I can read lips, you know," he answered. "You know the court dance at the finale? When they were dancing together, I saw Herb ask Joanie if she'd marry him, and when the next turn around came, she curtsied to him and said 'yes.'"

During the Christmas layoff of the 1947–48 tour, I took time off for the joyous wedding in Philadelphia, Mississippi. By the time the 1949 tour came around, they were joined by their two-month-old daughter.

While Bob rejoiced with all the Beatrices and Benedicts that Barter Theatre brought together, they only made him more painfully aware that his own marriage that had begun so happily beneath the apple blossoms of the Pocono Mountains was fading away. There were many reasons, of course, as there always are when two people who love one another begin to drift apart. The war had kept Bob and Fritz separated for more than two years, but thousands of other couples had been separated by the war and picked up their lives once it was over. No children had cemented the union, although Bob would have liked them. Whether Bob or Fritz could admit it at the time, however, the hard reality was that although he loved her deeply and sincerely and was devoted to her, Fritz was not Bob's first love. That was the Theatre, and as all too many people have discovered, that lover can be jealous and unforgiving.

> So far in this chronicle of my romance with the theatre I have dwelt upon the joys she gave me—the moments of rapture and the spangled pants. Even her hardships had yielded rewards, just as the joblessness of the Depression had brought forth Barter Theatre. But the stage is a demanding mistress as well as a satisfying one, time consuming and heart consuming. Antoinette Perry had called her a despot, a tyrant to whom you must be willing to pay tribute with every breathing moment of your life. To win her you must put no other god and no other loves before her.

As a young man Bob had been vulnerable to disillusion and always disappointed in people whom he believed had let him down. He learned to distrust ideals without the substance to back them up, and he easily saw through paper idols who were really, as he described them, façades with feet of clay. All through his life Bob had little patience with people who refused to grasp their bootstraps and at least try to pull themselves out of whatever bad situation they might be in. He didn't like quitters, and he had little use for those not willing to devote themselves to their goals as he devoted himself to his. At least in his mind he believed there was only one place and one universe where he could entrust his heart without fear of betrayal, and that place was the Theatre. It became the most important thing in his life, and, in fact, he later wrote that it became the most important thing, far and above his love for any man or woman. "I have been devoted to many people since," he said, "but always and only in proportion to the contribution they could make to the theatre—the Theatre as an institution and to my own Barter

Theatre in particular. It has been an all-absorbing selfishness," he admitted, "not for myself, but for my profession."

Fritz knew all of this at least on an intellectual level before she married Bob, and he—somewhat naively—believed she accepted it. At first perhaps she did, but in the end no human can be satisfied with being the lesser of two lovers. No doubt she was initially blinded by love and Bob Porterfield's charm as surely as he blind-ered himself to everything around him that did not in some way benefit his vision. Fritz devoted herself wholeheartedly to making her own contribution to the theatre, and she became a vital asset to Bob's dream. There is little doubt now that Barter Theatre would never have survived without her hard work, sacrifice, and financial acumen. She was a flawless business manager, forthright and as thrifty as her Pennsylvania Dutch forebears. Bob later said that he didn't realize how indispensable she was until after the war when he tried running the theatre and Barter Inn without her. As long as she had supervised the management of cafeteria and inn and box office, Bob could relax and go about his business of putting on plays and making friends for his theatre with the confidence that every penny was accounted for and every detail foreseen.

"Where, exactly, had things begun to go wrong?" Bob later won-dered. "Did my single-track devotion to the theatre cost Fritz more dearly than I was ever able to understand or acknowledge? Was it she, unwittingly, who paid the price for the fierce dedication that had made my theatre possible?"

Bob had grown up in a home where alcohol was not allowed in the days of Prohibition, but in New York he discovered that the Eighteenth Amendment only added to the fun and excitement of breaking the law. He accepted the theatre's ways in stride, but he could take liquor or leave it alone as he chose, and he mostly chose abstention. For him alcohol held neither allure nor opprobrium, and alcoholism, although at least as prevalent in the mountains of Virginia as elsewhere, was hardly recognized as a disease. Even though Bob did not necessarily agree with the idea, he had grown up around people who considered alcoholism a spiritual weakness that it was impolite to discuss.

Looking back on it now, my mind goes back to the Barter Award ceremony of 1941, the glittering occasion of Ethel Barrymore's luncheon in the star-studded Astor Ballroom. Fritz had taken charge of reservations and seating arrangements, tickets and food. I have said that she was a perfectionist, but it was more than that; though she handled every detail beautifully, she was one of those people who could never believe she had done anything right. The task of managing a banquet involving so many people and so many distinguished names overwhelmed her confidence. She fretted endlessly, lay awake at night trying to remember if there was anything she had forgotten. The luncheon that finally came off was a triumph of her wonderful ability, but even then she could not believe that she had indeed done everything to perfection, and she went to pieces. I remember it was the twelfth of May, our eighth wedding anniversary.

The situation baffled me. For the first time I was encountering a problem that could be met neither with a grin and a gift of gab, nor with the downright country logic of "taking the bull by the horns." I knew Fritz was high-strung and intense, afraid of having children, incapable of sitting still through even an act of a play, always moving to the back where she could stand or pace up and down.

On a visit to the Fritz family home in Bethlehem, in what Bob later called one of the ugliest scenes he had ever witnessed, Fritz's mother angrily turned on her daughter. "You're going to end up just like your father," she screamed. "It killed him, and it's going to kill you!"

Fritz turned pale. She had always been told the truth—that her father had died of pneumonia, but what she had not been told was that the pneumonia had been brought on by one of his lengthy bouts with delirium tremens. Alcohol had killed him.

Despite his personal agony in the late 1940s because of Fritz's rapidly declining health, Bob continued a full schedule of speaking engagements throughout the country. He fervently believed he had to keep promoting the idea of regional theatres and his own Barter Theatre, but much more on the practical side he knew the fees he earned for speaking were desperately needed to keep Barter going.

He tried to keep in touch with Fritz whenever he could, sometimes over the telephone but mostly by writing.

One day a letter from her caught up with him at the hotel in which he was staying. In shaky handwriting that had once been so neat and precise, she told Bob she was hospitalized for advanced cirrhosis. He immediately canceled two weeks of speaking commitments and headed to Pennsylvania. He found her very ill.

> Fritz was pensive and affectionate. Though she was still in her early forties, she spoke often of her death, and said that she would like to be buried in Virginia in the Porterfield family graveyard. She begged me not to leave, but one by one the days slipped by and I had to go.
>
> I was on the train going through Wilkes-Barre, Pennsylvania, when a great sense of foreboding came over me. I got off to call the hospital and find out how Fritz was. Her uncle was the one who told me she had just died. I told him of her wish to be buried in Virginia, but he grew angry and insisted that she be buried with the Fritzes in her own home state.

Although never divorced, Bob and Fritz had been legally separated on the advice of her doctor, who had told Bob that the separation "will either cure her or kill her." The uncle angrily informed Bob that his claim on Fritz was over. She was to be laid to rest in Pennsylvania, and nothing more was to be said. Bob heard the telephone being slammed down and then silence.

> I had a speaking engagement the next day. I remember still that it was in Elgin, Illinois, and there was barely enough time to get there. "The show must go on," I had said, more times than I can remember, but now I found that the adage could have a personal meaning.
>
> Numbly, I got back on the train. It was New Year's Day, 1949.

16

A Life beyond That of Mortals

Bob threw himself into the theatre even harder than ever after Fritz's death. It would be a long time before anyone would share her place in Bob's heart, although his old friend Alice Hilton did her best to fill Bob's need for a close friend and confidant.

James Hilton had received a hasty Mexican divorce from Alice in 1937 after only two years of marriage and then, just seven days later, married Galina Kopineck, a Hollywood starlet. After eight years of a tumultuous relationship with Kopineck, he divorced her as well. Despite all this, James, Alice, and Bob Porterfield remained solid friends. When James was diagnosed with cancer of the liver in 1953, Alice, although she had by then bought a home and permanently settled in Abingdon, went to his side in Long Beach, California, and nursed him lovingly until his death on December 20, 1954. Not only were James and Alice fully reconciled before he died, they became once again man and wife when they discovered that the divorce James had hastily acquired in Mexico had never been legal in the first place.

James Hilton had always loved Southwest Virginia because, he said, it reminded him of the English countryside where he was born. The man who had coined the magical word "Shangri-La" dreamed of someday moving to the hills of Virginia, but as a successful novelist and highly sought-after screenwriter, Hollywood held him captive in the very manner about which he had warned Bob. After his death, although he had been buried in California, his wish was finally granted; Alice and Bob saw to it that his body was disinterred and reburied in Abingdon in a cemetery plot that Bob owned.

Alice returned to Abingdon following James's death, and for the remainder of her own life she remained religiously devoted to Bob Porterfield, his theatre, and his dream—into all of which she poured her energy and resources. When she died on May 31, 1962, she was buried beside her husband. According to Anne St. Clair Williams: "The estate of the late James Hilton, which included a great deal of real estate in Abingdon and the literary rights to his novels, was left to his wife Alice for her lifetime, with a provision that the residue was to go to the Barter Theatre upon her death. Mrs. Hilton made her home with the Barter Company and served as Executive Secretary until her death . . . after which the assets of the Hilton estate were transferred to The Barter Foundation."

Despite all that was happening in his personal life and the complexity of running a rapidly growing theatrical operation as well as a model Grade A dairy farm, Bob never lost his desire to get in front of audiences and be a part of the magic he so loved. As one of Virginia's most famous ambassadors and promoters, it seems only right that the sole play in which he ever toured with Barter's players was, in 1951, *The Virginian*.

Many, including Bob, have considered Owen Wister's short novel as the first great American Western. *The Virginian* has been somewhat forgotten in the twenty-first century, but during the early 1950s virtually everyone had read the book, seen the play, or watched the movie. Given the title, its appearance on the Barter stage was inevitable.

Margaret Perry, the daughter of Antoinette Perry, had come to Barter as a director in 1950, and she convinced Bob quite easily that her next project should be *The Virginian*. What was not quite so easy was convincing him that he should star, but Margaret, a dynamo of energy whom Bob greatly admired, had made up her mind. "She twisted my arm, not very hard," he laughed, "and I found myself rehearsing the title role."

With all of his other responsibilities of running both a theatre with a staff of nearly one hundred and a dairy farm with a bovine contingent of almost that many, Bob discovered that he had little time left to study his script:

> I worried about being able to learn my "verses." I was a little bit
> too old for the leading part, and I've always said no other actor-

manager in his right mind would have let himself be starred alongside Chuck Quinlivan, one of the handsomest hunks of men currently on the television screen. I wore a corset trying to hold myself in, and Mack Statham, our set designer, said that he deserved a place in Barter history just because he laced it up for me every performance. The main thing the corset did was make me look chesty.

When I've finished admitting this, though, I have to say the whole adventure was a lark, and I loved every minute of it. I came into the theatre as an actor, and acting has always been my first love. *The Virginian* was one of those shows that is a romp to everyone around it. Everyone got into the act—even our caretaker, Colonel Sage, who played the role of a drunk more realistically than not, and my Irish setter Liza. Even the props and settings were fun—the electric train, the wagon in which we jiggled our way across the plains, and the famous Remington paintings of the old West which we had painted on glass and projected through slides on to the backdrop. On the opening night, the air was charged with electricity; we had the biggest audience the Barter Theatre had ever held. When I got out on stage and felt them in front of me, I was in my glory and I knew it.

The Virginian went on tour that autumn, and for Bob it was his first time doing one-night stands since Walter Hampden's *Cyrano*. He reveled in it all: the limelights, the fun, and the spirit of being on the road. For almost four months that Bob later described as the most pleasant he could remember, the tour rambled across the Old Dominion, Tennessee, Georgia, Alabama, Louisiana, Kentucky, and more.

I don't remember a lot of the place names, but I remember the audiences. I remember their variety, ever-changing; their warmth; their enthusiasm; their eagerness to fete us wherever we went. It was an unending round of socializing, performing, travel, and more socializing, night after night, but I don't remember being tired. There is nothing so exciting, so exhilarating as a live audience letting you know they like the show.

Bob regretted that he had not been able to keep up with acting, but his duties of running the theatre and all that it entailed had eclipsed everything else. Admittedly, he had gotten out of training. Actors are like athletes, he said. They have to stay in training if they want to keep up with the discipline and the concentration that their profession demands, and they have to be immune to distractions. Even during *The Virginian*, Bob said, he would sometimes look up and see a doorway standing open, and instead of listening to what the other actors were saying, he would fret about expensive air conditioning escaping into the humid summer night.

One evening, right in the middle of the play's famous frog scene, Bob glanced out into the audience and spotted his old friend Senator Harry Stuart sitting in the front row and making a remark to somebody near him. "I went up in my lines completely," said Bob, "and I couldn't hear what the prompter was whispering. I'd probably wallop any actor I saw doing this, but they tell me what I did was to walk over to where the prompt girl was sitting and ask, for everyone to hear, 'Huh, honey, huh?'"

Out of *The Virginian* tour came another one of Barter's favorite legends. It seems that the press agent was putting up a marquee in one town to announce "Robert Porterfield in *The Virginian*" when somebody shouted that he had a telephone call. He forgot, or so he later claimed, that he hadn't finished the marquee—which announced "Robert Porterfield in *The Virgin*." All Bob could do when he stopped laughing was to quote one of *The Virginian*'s most famous lines: "When you call me that, pardner—smile."

That was, unfortunately, the last acting Bob found time to enjoy. Even though he was approached to play the role of Big Daddy in *Cat on a Hot Tin Roof* in London, he knew he could never survive staying away from his theatre for so long. He at least partially satisfied his urge to perform by giving his famous curtain speeches at every Barter performance, a treat that Barter patrons eagerly anticipated. Some of his talks grew so long that the actors would poke him through the curtains so they could get on with the show. He also continued to push culture and speak to groups at every available chance—preferably, he said, to audiences of good people who might be tempted into a tax-deductible contribution to Barter Theatre.

Given his charisma and his speaking abilities, Bob was frequently asked why he did not run for public office. One day Walter Crockett, whose ancestor Davy had served as a Tennessee congressman before heading to the Alamo, and who was editor of the Bristol, Virginia/Tennessee newspapers at the time, proposed to Bob a run for Congress as a dark-horse candidate. With a wink, Bob told Crockett that he would run, but only if his platform could be "The Eternal Verities."

Crockett quoted Bob in the next day's paper, and all over Southwest Virginia and East Tennessee dusty dictionaries and encyclopedias were dragged out and studiously perused. Supporting letters-to-the-editor poured in, but Bob and Crockett laughingly called off the campaign a day or two later because it seemed that nobody knew or could agree on just what the eternal verities are.

The first New York theatre in which Bob had ever performed was the grand old Empire. On this theatre's stage, first opened on January 25, 1893, Bob had acted as part of his training with the American Academy of Dramatic Arts. In fact, the stage of the Empire was where he had flubbed his attempt at a British accent and had accepted the reality that he just plain talked "Virginian" and that people could either like his accent or not as they chose. So it was with a very real sense of loss that Bob received word in 1953 that the venerable old theatre was to be closed and the building demolished to make way for a modern nineteen-story, air-conditioned office tower. The Empire had been the first of the great theatres to move northward from Herald Square, and now it was the last of its kind, all alone and struggling for life on Broadway and Fortieth Street, abandoned by the fashionable set that had by then moved uptown. Gone was the Knickerbocker, the Casino, the Comedy, the Princess, and the Garrick; soon, gone too would be the Empire, despite a hopeless last-minute attempt to save it.

But what preservationists were not able to accomplish, Bob Porterfield could — at least in part. The Astor family had owned the building since 1946, and at the urging of an attorney who was a mutual acquaintance, Lady Astor agreed to give Bob everything he could remove from the theatre that he thought might be useful at Barter. The only problem was that the demolition company already had a contract in hand to level the building and no desire to stand by with diesels idling and union laborers drawing overtime while a gaggle of theatre people from somewhere in Virginia picked over curtains, lights, and other such thespian frippery. After the old the-atre's last performance (*The Time of the Cuckoo*) Bob was to be al-lowed only two days to rip out, unscrew, dismount, salvage, and cart off as much as he could. After that the wrecking ball and bull-dozers would move in blitzkrieg-style and crush to rubble every-thing that remained.

"At the final curtain call," said Bob, "Edna Wallace Hopper stood on one side of the stage and Shirley Booth on the other, and between them in the silence stood the ghosts of all the Empire's great play-ers who had trod its boards in the sixty years between. In the bare work light, the curtain rose and fell three times."

Bob's personal cash reserves were almost nonexistent as were those of Barter, since it was just a week before the summer season was due to begin in Abingdon and every available nickel had al-ready been spent in preparation. Bob and Barter, however, had an informal but very loyal alumni club in New York composed of people who had been somehow touched by one or both. When this group heard of the chance to rescue a part of the Empire and transplant it to Abingdon, Bob's underground rose to the occa-sion. Former Barter actors and actresses whose names are now known throughout the theatre, television, and movie worlds, along with dozens of people who were comfortably anonymous, linked arms to make the near-impossible happen and to keep a little of the magic alive.

Gossip began buzzing at Sardi's and other restaurants frequented by show people, telephones began to ring, and word spread like wildfire that the indefatigable Bob Porterfield and his Old Domin-ion cavalry were riding to rescue as much as they could of the Em-pire. When Bob's electrician and technical coordinator arrived in New York ahead of everyone else, they found a full-sized crew was already on hand dressed in work clothes and armed with hammers, crowbars, and assorted other wrecking tools.

> In the two-day race against the deadline working around the clock to untack carpeting, dismount brass and crystal chande-liers, dismantle seats and balcony rails and dimmer boards, the actors never stopped coming. Some of them could stay only an

hour or two, long enough to unscrew a row of seats or pack away a panel of precious damask, and swap memories of a Barter tour. Some of them came between performances of a Broadway play, between rehearsals, or during an office lunch hour. But by the morning of June 2, when the bulldozers arrived on the scene, the stars and stagehands, ad-writers and office girls had dismantled three oversize van loads of richly cushioned seats, wall sconces, brass door rings and orchestra rails, chandeliers and miles of red carpeting. Last to be loaded were the front curtain with its golden "E" embossed on crimson, and the doorman's coat with its golden epaulettes. The crew disappeared as quickly as it had assembled, and as the truck drivers pulled their vans out on to Broadway, the last sound they could hear were the pneumatic drills breaking up the marble floors that had been the Empire's lobby.

All of the Empire salvage was free, and except for some food and lodging expenses so was the crew, but the cost of employing three large Mason-Dixon Trucking Company tractor-trailers and their drivers was anything but. As the season had not yet generated any cash flow and resources were tight, Bob turned to what he called his "In the Hole" committee for financial help. This loose-knit group included everyone from Mary Chase who wrote *Harvey* to Helen Hayes, Eleanor Roosevelt, one of Abingdon's local undertakers, and many others, who, of course, immediately pledged enough donations to foot Bob's sizable haul bill.

The truck drivers made all possible haste, but even at that they arrived in Abingdon only two days before our twenty-first season was scheduled to open. We made that deadline, too; don't ask me how. On the opening night 398 Empire seats replaced our wooden chairs. The Empire damask, bracketed with brass and dripping with crystal prisms, gave a new depth and luster to our walls, and the curtain that rose on the new season bore the gilded "E."

Bob had invited Ward King, the president of Mason-Dixon — whose motto was "We Cover Dixie like the Dew" — to attend Barter on opening night. He had visited the theatre several times in the past, but when he spied the almost miraculous transformation that had taken place in only two days, he was overwhelmed. As he congratulated everyone involved on their accomplishment, he calmly pulled the thick Mason-Dixon trucking bill out of his coat pocket, but instead of presenting it to Bob for payment, he calmly ripped the bill into several pieces and declared it paid in full. When Bob tried to refund the money given to him by his "In the Hole" committee, the contributors refused to take it back and insisted that Bob use the money for one of his long-cherished dreams: air conditioning for the theatre.

> Some of the damask from the Empire's walls was left over. My mother took pieces of it and made them into pin cushions, stuffed with the wool of my Glade Springs sheep. I sent them to all the great leading ladies who had sat at the Empire's star dressing room table, knowing they would want some memento of the old playhouse, and many of them wrote in their letters of gratitude that they sat down and wept at the sight of that scrap of memory.
>
> I admit to being prejudiced, but I think there is something very appropriate in the Empire's final destination. Tradition means a lot to me, and I like to think of having joined the Empire's tradition to Abingdon's own tradition of a rugged pioneer spirit. In one of the old brick homes on its Main Street is a carefully preserved piece of stump, found not far away, bearing a legend: "D. Boone killed a Bear." D. Boone actually did record in his journals going through the community as he pressed westward along the Wilderness Road. . . . Abingdon is a living town, committed to the present, but its memories are rooted in the past.

Even though Barter Theatre, like nearly all arts organizations throughout history, was constantly in need of funds to keep the lights on, both Bob Porterfield and Barter were beginning to take on the luster—or the tarnish—of senior statesmen. Bob was named First Citizen of Abingdon in 1957 and presented the Actors' Fund Award of Merit that same year. In 1963, he received the Thomas Jefferson Award for public relations on behalf of Virginia. In 1967, the Suzanne Davis Memorial Award for contributions to theatre in the South was awarded to him, as was the Special Service Award from the Virginia State Chamber of Commerce. He also founded the Washington County Public Library because he firmly believed that education was the key to prosperity, and a good library one of the pillars of education. Eddie Yates, who went on to become a very successful businessman and world traveler, relates that once, when he was a boy, he was coming out of the library when he met Bob Porterfield, whom he of course recognized. Bob pointed to the books under Eddie's arm and said, "Son, those will take you places." Eddie never forgot.

Magazines and newspapers all over the United States—indeed, throughout much of the world—published articles about Bob and his theatre. Famous actors, directors, and playwrights communicated with Bob regularly, and some, such as Tennessee Williams, used the Barter stage to premiere new works—in the case of Williams, a revised version of his play *The Milk Train Doesn't Stop Here Anymore.* In 1957, Ernest Borgnine was featured on the popular television show *This Is Your Life,* and of course Bob and Barter were featured prominently. Former Barter actors who had gravitated to the movies received Oscars: Gregory Peck in 1963, and in 1964 Patricia Neal. Diane Cilento, also a former Barter player, was nominated for an Oscar in 1964 for Best Supporting Actress.

A list of the other Barter alumni who were either discovered or encouraged by Bob Porterfield and who went on to become well-known includes Mitch Ryan, Claude Akins, Rosemary Murphy, Fritz Weaver, Ned Beatty, Larry Linville, and many others.

Not everything went Bob's way every day, of course. Like anyone he had his setbacks, his little squabbles with the Abingdon Town Council, personnel who simply didn't work out, and all the other busted water pipes of life. But he never let any of them destroy his optimism and his zest for life and for the Theatre.

Bob realized, also, that past laurels are no place to rest. If anything, accolades only made it more difficult to keep the spark of creativity and innovation burning brightly. It would have been easy to coast, at least for a few years, on reputation and the production of "safe" plays featuring established actors, but Bob had never gone that route and he wasn't about to now. He relished his reputation as a producer willing to give promising newcomers—actors, writers, and all the others—a chance to prove themselves, and he enjoyed challenges. Still, as the years began to roll by faster and faster he began to project the fate of his Barter Theatre in the years to come, especially the years following his death. He was still a young man in his mid-fifties, and for once he seems not to have had any premonition of danger, or, if he did, he doesn't appear to have dwelt upon it or to have shared it with anyone. His beloved mother, Miss Daisy, had passed away in 1955, which surely must have brought home to Bob thoughts of his own mortality. For years Miss Daisy had continued to live at Twin Oaks, but as her health declined she had moved to an apartment at the Barter Inn to be close to Bob. In a May 17, 1967, conversation with Anne St. Clair Williams, however, Bob said the thing that prompted him to really begin considering Barter Theatre's future without him was the death of Margo Jones and the subsequent collapse of her Dallas theatre. This made him realize, Bob told Williams, that to that date no regional theatre had long outlived its founder. He was determined that Barter Theatre would be different, and he believed that to survive it had to always be Barter Theatre, never a memorial to Robert Porterfield.

> I want to perpetuate the dream and make it multiply. Keep theatre in the Virginia Highlands as a mirror of truth as it was and is and should be, and make it last longer than one man's lifespan. In other words, defeat the old antagonist of Time.
>
> Is it impossible? No one in this country has managed to do it yet. Theatrical empires have risen, and the Frohmans, the Ziegfields, the David Belascos, and the Jed Harrises have had their day, but never have their works outlived the founders. Margo Jones had a great dream for a theatre in Dallas, and she fulfilled her dream with a vital, exciting theatre. Then one day I read in the newspaper that Margo Jones had died, and the next year the Margo Jones Theatre was dead.
>
> Will that happen to Barter Theatre? I'd like to think not. I'd like to think my work is not as mortal as myself. I'm hanging on to Saint Rita in the hopes that Barter Theatre will prove to be more than bricks and mortar, and that what it is will outlast me and my generation, perhaps even the next generation and the one after that.

During the spring of 1962, the Old Dominion Foundation offered Barter a one-hundred-thousand-dollar grant to consolidate its resources and establish a perpetuating foundation to help ensure the theatre's survival. The foundation offered its grant on condition that Bob raise another twenty-five thousand dollars in matching funds from local individuals and that the board of directors be reorganized so that it would have more direct contact with the theatre's operations. Bob had always liked to have a board of directors that pretty much kept its hands off day-to-day operations, but he was also practical. The Barter Foundation was incorporated in July 1962 as a "non-profit, tax-exempt corporation engaged in literary, educational and cultural activities," and by October Bob had raised more than thirty thousand dollars to match the Old Dominion grant funds. Bob, his new board of directors, and the Commonwealth of Virginia all seemed determined to give Barter a life of its own that would continue beyond the "four score and seven" allotted to mortals.

Bob and his mother, Miss Daisy, at Twin Oaks.

17

He Loved the Theatre, Loved His Fellow Man, and Loved Virginia

Perhaps it was his Cherokee intuition, perhaps all the talk of continuing Barter Theatre after his death, or maybe it was just the fact that creative minds are more keenly aware of human mortality than are those of a less thoughtful bent, but Bob now appeared ready to relinquish a substantial amount of control over the theatre he had created—and to allow it a little less control over his own personal life. Many of the people he had loved and admired the most had passed on: his father, Fritz, Miss Daisy, James Hilton, Alice Hilton in 1962, and Charles Vance in 1963.

Following Vance's death, Mary Dudley closed up the couple's house—they by then had removed themselves from the antiques business—and temporarily moved back to her girlhood home in Bolton, Mississippi, to, in her words, "be with my parents until I could decide the direction of the rest of my life."

Not too long afterward, however, she picked up the ringing telephone and heard a pleasantly familiar baritone voice. Bob Porterfield told her he had been given a six-month grant to start a "Friends of Barter" project that he hoped to persuade her to return to Abingdon and organize. The Friends was a group of men and women who among other things promoted ticket sales in each town to which Barter's troupe traveled.

She was reluctant to move back to Abingdon with its many memories of Charlie, and she feared the thought of living alone, but Bob was persistent. He called her and wrote and, on the fifth or

Mary Dudley and Bob Porterfield.

sixth of his entreaties, she agreed. When the job as Friends organizer ended after six months, she accepted a position as secretary with the Washington County Chamber of Commerce. Since the chamber's office was in the same building as the Barter Theatre, she and Bob saw one another almost every day, and their friendship deepened. On October 6, 1964, she and Bob were married at noon in her hometown of Bolton, Mississippi. By then, Bob had bought out his brothers' share of Twin Oaks, and he and his new wife settled there. For Bob, it was the first time in many years that he did not live at the Barter Inn, and the old farm seemed to satisfy his growing need for permanence and roots. Other than a minor heart attack in 1965 his health was good, and his favorite clothing when he was not involved in theatre business became the working garb of a family farmer. He did not encourage Mary Dudley to participate in the theatre's operations because, she said, he loved having his new wife at home when he came in after a hard day of work. He also loved entertaining beneath the huge oaks, often rather on the spur of the moment, and sometimes his spontaneous invitations landed him in hot water.

Mary Dudley relates that at an après-drama party one Saturday night people suddenly began coming up to her and thanking her for inviting them to Twin Oaks for brunch the following morning. After this occurred several times, Mary Dudley buttonholed Bob and demanded to know what was going on and why he was inviting people to a brunch of which she had no knowledge.

"What am I going to feed all those people?" she quizzed him.

"Oh, I'm certain you'll manage," he assured her with confidence.

Somehow or other just after sunup she found a small country grocery store open and managed to buy enough eggs, bacon, bread, and other essentials to feed everyone, none of whom realized what a Herculean task she had accomplished on such short notice.

Despite his newfound love of permanence and home, Bob's commitment to promoting regional theatre throughout the country remained very much in his mind. On March 8, 1966, he and the producers of twenty-five other regional theatres met in New York and organized the League of Resident Theatres, which, among other things, was to be a bargaining entity for negotiations with the Actors' Equity Association and other unions.

In late 1965 Bob decided that the time had come to trust day-to-day operations of Barter to Peter Culman, who had managed all aspects of Barter's operation under Bob's supervision during the 1964 and 1965 seasons. Culman was executive vice president of The Barter Foundation, associate producer, production coordinator, and, increasingly, Bob's handpicked choice of a successor. Culman was

Bob at home with Dobbin and a feline friend.

Bob and Jay at Twin Oaks. The two were more than just father and son; they were good friends.

put completely in charge of the season, and Bob and Mary Dudley embarked on an extended vacation tour of Europe. Even though the trip was technically a vacation, the couple naturally visited theatres in Spain, Portugal, France, Italy, England, Ireland, and everywhere else their travels took them.

It was a wonderful and memorable trip, but when Bob returned to Abingdon he found that, according to Anne St. Clair Williams:

> During the summer, Culman had ordered all storage areas cleaned. Out came properties: furniture, some rare antiques included, that had been collected through the years; draperies and pictures; hand properties; and many relics and souvenirs, as well as some of Porterfield's personal belongings stored at the Barter Inn. Culman left bare what had been, according to Bob, a "veritable treasure house" when he ordered twenty-five truckloads of items hauled to the town dump.

Roxie McCracken and William White, maid and janitor at the Barter Inn, told Williams that Culman ordered them to haul away a large canvas painting that had been given to Bob and which had hung in the hallway at the Barter Inn. Loyal to Bob and knowing that he was fond of the painting, the two of them defied Culman's orders and saved the painting by hiding it in the janitor's bathroom in the basement.

Also, according to Williams, the season ended on October 2, 1966, with the largest deficit in Barter's history. Bob dismissed Culman and once again began trying to find a person who he could feel was the right individual to take over Barter's reins. Although Culman didn't become Bob's successor at the Barter, the lessons he learned there doubtlessly played a major part in his very successful theatrical career as managing director of Center Stage in Baltimore, one of America's premiere theatres.

Bob also had no heirs to whom he could leave Twin Oaks. He had always wanted a son, but neither of his marriages had produced either a son or daughter. In 1968 he and Mary Dudley adopted a five-year-old boy they named Jay Payne Porterfield. He and Bob quickly became very close, and "Jay Bird," as Bob liked to call him, provided Bob with some of the most pleasant moments of his life.

Bob frequently mentioned his new son in the famous "Groundhog Day Letters" that he composed every year and mailed to select friends. These missives were eagerly awaited and included accounts of what Bob and his family and the various people and animals living at Twin Oaks had been up to during the past twelve months and, of course, plenty of news about goings-on at Barter during the past season. Frequently they were adorned with little sketches of woodchucks, cows, or whatever else happened to be on Bob's mind at the time. Bob only mailed these highly prized letters to people who had sent him a Christmas card in the previous holiday season. The only eccentricity was that Bob himself never mailed out Christmas cards.

Despite the Culman episode and his heart attack, Bob seemed to be enjoying life more and more with every passing season. He took tremendous pride in the Twin Oaks Grade-A dairy farm, enjoyed long walks and father-to-son discussions with Jay as well as romping with the family's huge Irish wolfhound. Mary Dudley recalled those times for the Historical Society of Washington County, Virginia, in a newsletter article:

> Bob and I both loved dogs, so when he came home from a Virginia Travel Council meeting in northern Virginia and told me that a friend of his had given him a registered Irish wolfhound, I was delighted. The dog had been shipped by air from Ireland when it was a small puppy; it had now outgrown its doghouse and yard and needed to live on a farm.
>
> The wolfhound's registered name was "Lewis of Ballinaboy," but we called him Dobbin. From the very minute he was brought to Twin Oaks, he was Bob's dog. He followed Bob's every footstep and was with him every possible minute. Wolfhounds are known for their loyalty and affection for one person. Dobbin tolerated the rest of us at the farm, but Bob was his master. He won first prize in the Virginia Highlands Festival Dog Show so many times that Bob decided not to show him anymore.
>
> Dobbin was a big dog. One day Bob had to go into Glade Spring, and Dobbin jumped in the back seat of the car to go along. At the railroad crossing not far from Twin Oaks, they waited for a train to pass, but the engineer stopped the train right at the crossing. "Bob," said the engineer, "I told myself if I

ever got near enough to you and saw that animal of yours, I was going to stop this train and see for myself what it was." Bob knew the engineer. He and the dog got out of the car so the man could meet Dobbin. As the engineer started back to the train, he said, "Well, he's a dog, but he sure could pass for a calf."

Together, Bob and Mary Dudley worked to restore the beautiful old brick home at Twin Oaks, adding a front patio and doing many other improvements and repairs. The giant oaks grew more majestic each year, and although their life together was often exhilarating, the couple frequently had quiet times and made many wonderful memories together during the next few years. Mary Dudley remembered that it was for all the world like a wonderful fairytale.

Even a serious automobile accident failed to dampen Bob's happiness and enthusiasm for life. In 1968, returning from a speaking engagement at Carson-Newman College near Knoxville, a drunken driver slammed into the driver's side of the couple's car, injuring Bob badly and causing physical problems that eventually led to a hip replacement. The injury and subsequent pain seemed to cause Bob's health to deteriorate, but he tried to continue as he always had although it was obvious to everyone, especially his wife, that he needed to slow down a little. Hip replacement surgery not too long after the accident, however, seemed to improve his health and feeling of well-being, so much so that he declared he felt better than he had for a long time, even before the accident.

In early October 1971, Bob insisted on attending a play in Washington, D.C., and then visiting New York despite suffering from a bad cold that seemed determined to develop into pneumonia. Mary Dudley tried to convince him to stay in Virginia but to no avail, and the two of them flew to Washington and traveled on to New York. By the time they arrived home by plane, Bob's cold had indeed become far more serious. He became more ill during the next few days and ended up in Johnston Memorial Hospital's intensive care unit in Abingdon on October 22, just two days before Barter's final presentation of the season. Not long after sunrise on the morning of October 28, 1971, Robert H. Porterfield's heart that had loved the theatre, loved his fellow man, and loved Virginia, beat its last. He was sixty-five.

18

The Good Earth

Bob Porterfield's body, in a simple brown casket of solid Appalachian red oak, was brought home to Twin Oaks for his funeral on the afternoon of October 29, 1971. A single spray of yellow autumn mums decorated its top. The huge oaks that he had loved so well were still ablaze with fall color and cascaded their leaves onto Bob's casket as if, Mrs. Porterfield later wrote, the ancient trees were weeping. Dobbin lay on the ground at his master's feet during the service. Three months later he, too, would pass away. The only possible explanation for his death, the veterinarian said, was grief for the man he had loved so deeply.

Praise for Bob and his work came in from all over the world: from congressmen, famous actors and actresses, the governor of Virginia, and President Richard Nixon, who personally telephoned Mary Dudley. But it would have been the outpouring of condolences from the local mountain people, the farmers and laborers and the planters-of-rows-of-extra-beans, that Bob Porterfield would surely have cherished most.

The *Bristol Herald Courier* in an editorial spoke for many:

> All of those who knew Bob Porterfield will miss him deeply. And it will not be possible for any of us to visit Barter without hearing again his laughter, without remembering his welcoming remarks from the stage, without recalling something of what he was and what he gave to all of us.

Bob was laid to rest beside James and Alice Hilton, two people he loved dearly and who loved him, and there is still room for his cherished wife Mary Dudley Porterfield when eventually the time comes that it is needed. It is a shady spot beneath large trees and within sight of the Wilderness Road. Thousands of people hurry by every day, but few of them know that two of America's most famous dreamers—James Hilton and Robert Porterfield—sleep peacefully just a few feet up the hill.

As the final words of the ceremony faded away into the mountainsides resplendent in their late October finery, Bob's casket was gently lowered into the earth of Virginia, the rich soil that had nourished and grown the world of wonder he had created out of magic and dreams and spangled pants. High overhead, a lone raven, with sunset-glistening ebony wings outstretched to catch the warm autumn updraft, soared in graceful ascending spirals, growing smaller and smaller until it disappeared.

Epilogue: The Dream Lives On

There'll never be another Bob Porterfield

As he hoped and had faith that it would, Bob Porterfield's Barter Theatre lives on more than thirty-five years after his passing. It is stronger than ever, yet it still continues Bob's tradition of providing hard, intensive repertory work for young and aspiring actors and actresses, of producing "well-cured hams."

Thanks to the vision of Barter's Board of Trustees, Rex Partington, an experienced theatre professional familiar with Bob's philosophy and who had actually worked at Barter with Bob, was selected to carry on Bob's work as producer and artistic director. Partington would have been the first to state that he could not fill Bob's gigantic shoes, but he successfully proved himself to be a strong and creative individual brave enough to tackle what was, he told Mary Dudley, the hardest role of his career. He was followed two decades later by Richard Rose, who has successfully piloted Barter into the twenty-first century by both honoring tradition and blazing new trails.

After Bob's funeral, the dairy employees approached Mary Dudley and asked her, "What are we going to do now?"

"What do you think we are going to do?" she asked. "We're going to keep right on running this farm!" And that is exactly what she and her hands did for several years afterward. For Mary Dudley, throwing herself into the farm was a way of coping with the death of a man she did and still does love dearly. The agricultural operation has since been leased to a neighboring farmer who raises beef cattle. The Grade-A dairy cows are gone, but as of this writing Mary Dudley still resides at Twin Oaks and still entertains a few visitors with grace and charm amid portraits and memorabilia of Bob.

Jay Porterfield, who did not make a career of the theatre, still lives in Southwest Virginia, as does his son—and Bob's grandson—Robert, and Bob's great-grandson, Dylan Alexander Porterfield.

In addition to classic plays and musicals, Barter still goes out of its way to stage the works of new and relatively unknown playwrights and to draw upon the rich legacy of Bob Porterfield's beloved mountains. As in Bob's day, some of the productions arouse controversy, and although open ostracism of Theatre people has pretty much disappeared from the hills and hollows and tree-lined streets, a few preachers do still remember to offer up a prayer now and then for the souls of people in "that wicked show business."

And in ongoing tribute to Bob Porterfield, Barter Theatre's present producing artistic director still offers the founder's traditional intonation at the close of the curtain speech welcoming a new generation of theatre patrons:

> "If you like us, talk about us. And if you don't, just keep your mouth shut."

Index

Numbers in *italics* indicate photographs.

About the Author

 Robert McKinney holds a bachelor of science degree in forestry from West Virginia University and a master of professional writing degree from the University of Southern California. He is an active member of the Outdoor Writers Association of America and a senior contributing editor for *Sporting Classics* magazine. He has been reviewing theatre for the *Bristol Herald Courier* for more than a decade. A native Southwest Virginian, he is an award-winning freelance writer and photographer who lives beside the South Fork of the Holston River near Sugar Grove with his first wife, assorted wild and domestic critters, seven bicycles, a John Deere, a Harley, the requisite pickup truck, and an old TR-6 he is restoring.